BestMasters

Mit **„BestMasters“** zeichnet Springer die besten Masterarbeiten aus, die an renommierten Hochschulen in Deutschland, Österreich und der Schweiz entstanden sind. Die mit Höchstnote ausgezeichneten Arbeiten wurden durch Gutachter zur Veröffentlichung empfohlen und behandeln aktuelle Themen aus unterschiedlichen Fachgebieten der Naturwissenschaften, Psychologie, Technik und Wirtschaftswissenschaften. Die Reihe wendet sich an Praktiker und Wissenschaftler gleichermaßen und soll insbesondere auch Nachwuchswissenschaftlern Orientierung geben.

Springer awards **“BestMasters”** to the best master’s theses which have been completed at renowned Universities in Germany, Austria, and Switzerland. The studies received highest marks and were recommended for publication by supervisors. They address current issues from various fields of research in natural sciences, psychology, technology, and economics. The series addresses practitioners as well as scientists and, in particular, offers guidance for early stage researchers.

Maximilian Markus Grossmann

Blockchain-Based Bonds

A Game Changer in Corporate Financing?

Springer Gabler

Maximilian Markus Grossmann
Blockchain Center
Frankfurt School of Finance & Management
Frankfurt, Germany

ISSN 2625-3577 ISSN 2625-3615 (electronic)
BestMasters
ISBN 978-3-658-45310-7 ISBN 978-3-658-45311-4 (eBook)
https://doi.org/10.1007/978-3-658-45311-4

This Springer Gabler imprint is published by the registered company Springer Fachmedien Wiesbaden GmbH, part of Springer Nature.
The registered company address is: Abraham-Lincoln-Str. 46, 65189 Wiesbaden, Germany

Abstract

This study delves into the impact of blockchain-based bonds on corporate financing and the bond market, with a specific focus on Germany. Utilizing qualitative insights from 19 experts, it compares blockchain-based bonds with traditional bonds, explores market-adoption dynamics, assesses the evolving roles of market intermediaries, and considers future development prospects. The findings suggest that blockchain-based bonds could offer long-term benefits in terms of accessibility, overall risk, cost efficiency, and transparency. However, they currently face significant challenges, including technological fragmentation, high liquidity risks, large investment requirements, and regulatory complexities. Market adoption is still in its nascent stages, with development initiatives like the DLT Pilot Regime not yet making a substantial impact. The study also highlights a potential shift in the roles of market intermediaries in the blockchain era, indicating new functions and possible obsolescence for some traditional roles. Experts offer varied predictions for the future of blockchain-based bonds, from the possibility of replacing traditional bonds to serving as complementary solutions or being superseded by other digital approaches. The study concludes that while blockchain-based bonds hold considerable potential for transforming the financial sector, their full adoption and impact depend on overcoming current challenges and adapting to the evolving regulatory and overall market dynamics.

Keywords: Blockchain-based bonds · Corporate financing · DLT · Financial markets transformation · Fintech

Contents

Abbreviations

AI	Artificial intelligence
AML	Anti-money laundering
BaFin	*Bundesanstalt fuer Finanzdienstleistungsaufsicht* [Federal Financial Supervisory Authority]
BCBS	Basel Committee on Banking Supervision
BTC	Bitcoin
CBDC	Central Bank Digital Currency
CBECI	Cambridge Bitcoin Energy Consumption Index
CCP	Central counterparty
COVID-19	Coronavirus disease 2019
CSD	Central Securities Depository
CSDR	Central Securities Depositories Regulation
dApp	Decentralized application
DLT	Distributed ledger technology
DvP	Delivery versus payment
e.g.	*Exempli gratia* [for example]
ECB	European Central Bank
EIB	European Investment Bank
EMIR	European Market Infrastructure Regulation
ESG	Environmental, social and governance
ESMA	European Securities and Markets Authority
ETH	Ether
EU	European Union
EUGB	European Union green bonds

EVM	Ethereum Virtual Machine
eWpG	*Gesetz ueber elektronische Wertpapiere* [German Electronic Securities Act]
eWpRV	*Verordnung ueber Anforderungen an elektronische Wertpapierregister* [Ordinance on Requirements on Electronic Securities Registers]
Fintech	Financial technology
FMI	Financial market infrastructure
GB	Gigabyte
ICO	Initial coin offering
i.e.	*Id est* [that is]
IoT	Internet of things
KWG	*Kreditwesengesetz* [German Banking Act]
KYC	Know your customer
MB	Megabyte
MiCA	Markets in Crypto-Assets Regulation
MiFID	Markets in Financial Instruments Directive
MiFIR	Markets in Financial Instruments Regulation
MTF	Multilateral trading facilities
NFT	Non-fungible token
OTC	Over-the-counter
P2P	Peer-to-peer
PoS	Proof of stake
PoW	Proof of work
RQ	Research question
SegWit	Segregated Witness
SME	Small and medium-sized enterprises
SPV	Simplified payment verification
SS	Settlement systems
TSS	Trading and settlement systems
TWh	Terawatt hour
UK	United Kingdom
U.S.	United States of America
y-o-y	Year-over-year

List of Figures

List of Tables

Introduction 1

1.1 Background and Motivation

In recent years, the financial landscape has undergone a substantial transformation, driven by a series of technological advancements and the introduction of innovative instruments. This evolution has been marked by several key developments, each contributing significantly to the reshaping of the financial sector's dynamics.

The emergence of mobile banking and payment platforms stands as an important milestone in this transformation, fundamentally changing how financial transactions are conducted. These platforms have democratized access to financial services, thereby contributing to a more inclusive global financial system (Alt et al., 2018). Subsequently, the integration of big data and analytics into finance has enabled institutions to enhance decision-making and risk assessments as well as to offer personalized services, leading to more efficient and customer-centric solutions (Hasan et al., 2020).

The incorporation of artificial intelligence (AI) has marked another notable progression. AI, particularly in the form of predictive analytics, has enhanced forecasting capabilities for market trends and company performance. Additionally, its application in algorithmic trading, leveraging the ability to process and analyze vast datasets, has revolutionized trading decisions, heralding a new era in financial markets (Cohen, 2022).

In the dynamic landscape of financial innovation, blockchain technology has emerged as a particularly transformative force. Initially recognized for its role in cryptocurrencies, the scope of blockchain's applications has expanded significantly. Notable among these applications are supply chain finance solutions, which facilitate early invoice payments for suppliers and extend payment terms

M. M. Grossmann, *Blockchain-Based Bonds*, BestMasters,
https://doi.org/10.1007/978-3-658-45311-4_1

for buyers (Zhang et al., 2021), and initial coin offerings (ICOs), where companies raise capital by issuing tokens or coins (Adhami et al., 2018). However, it is the impact on securities trading that has recently garnered substantial attention, particularly in Germany since February 2023.

At this time, Siemens—as of January 12, 2024, the second-largest company in Germany by market capitalization (Bloomberg, 2024)—made a notable move by issuing a corporate bond with a volume of €60 million, not through traditional channels, but through the Polygon blockchain network. This issuance, a first for one of the 40 companies in Germany's DAX stock-market index, involved the direct sale of securities to major investors such as DekaBank, DZ Bank, and Union Investment, bypassing traditional securities depositories (Siemens, 2023). This approach was not merely a milestone in corporate financing; instead, it represented a robust endorsement of blockchain technology's practicality and reliability. Siemens's decision marked a significant moment in the German corporate financing landscape and highlighted the growing confidence in the practical applications of blockchain technology in corporate finance.

The integration of blockchain technology into the bond market represents a notable development in financial innovation. This technology challenges traditional practices and introduces possibilities for broader access and increased transparency. The bond market, which has historically depended on conventional mechanisms, is now encountering a disruptive force in the form of blockchain. This shift could mark a significant evolution in corporate financing methods, potentially leading to a more inclusive and transparent financial landscape.

1.2 Objectives of the Study and Research Questions

While the potential of blockchain-based bonds has also garnered increasing attention in academic circles, most existing literature remains theoretical, offering limited insight into real-world applications and perspectives from practitioners. However, the dynamic nature of blockchain technology requires close alignment between theoretical exploration and practical implementation. This paper endeavors to bridge this gap, giving insights into the opinions and experiences of experts working with the opportunities that blockchain offers in the bond market.

The objective of this research is to provide a comprehensive analysis of blockchain-based bonds, contrasting them with traditional bonds to elucidate their features and potential advantages or disadvantages. By exploring the benefits and challenges as well as the evolving roles of market intermediaries in the context of blockchain adoption, this research aims to build a nuanced understanding of how blockchain technology might revolutionize or disrupt the current bond market. As such, it should assist bond issuers, investors, and policymakers in navigating this emerging field, while also enhancing the academic dialogue by uncovering research opportunities stemming from practical experiences.

Central to this study is the main research question (RQ): "What impact do blockchain-based bonds have on corporate financing, and how can they change the setup in the bond market?" To comprehensively address this question, the research is structured around four subordinate research questions:

RQ1: How do blockchain-based bonds compare to traditional bonds in terms of accessibility, risk, cost, and transparency?

RQ2: What are the perceived benefits of, and key barriers to, blockchain-based bonds, and what are current market-adoption dynamics?

RQ3: How can blockchain technology transform the roles and functions of market intermediaries and infrastructure providers in the context of bond markets?

RQ4: How do experts assess the future development of blockchain-based bonds?

Employing a qualitative research methodology, this study draws upon insights from 19 experts across banking, fintech, corporate finance, and asset management. With a particular focus on the German market, these interviews provide a rich, in-depth perspective on the nuances and intricacies of blockchain-based bonds.

1.3 Structure

The structure of the paper is designed to support an objective and extensive exploration of blockchain-based bonds and their impact on corporate financing and the bond market.

Chapter 2 explores the theoretical background of the study, delving into the means of corporate financing with a particular focus on bonds, blockchain technology, and the concept of blockchain-based bonds. The fundamentals of blockchain technology are explored in depth to accommodate readers with different levels of expertise in this area. Understanding these basics is considered essential to appreciate the opportunities and challenges that blockchain introduces in the bond market.

Chapter 3 outlines the study's methodology, describing the expert interview approach, sample selection, questionnaire design, interview process, and analysis methods. It also details the quality criteria employed to maintain research integrity.

Chapter 4 presents the analysis of the qualitative data gathered and is structured systematically in line with the research questions. It encompasses a comparison with traditional bonds from different perspectives; the benefits of, and implementation barriers to, blockchain-based bonds; market-adoption dynamics; and the transformation of intermediary and infrastructure-provider roles. The chapter concludes with an outlook on standards and prospects for blockchain-based bonds.

Chapter 5 summarizes the results to answer the subordinate research questions. Moreover, it discusses the results with reference to the related literature.

The paper concludes with Chapter 6, which presents a summary of the findings, proposes directions for future research, and discusses both theoretical and practical implications. Additionally, it acknowledges the study's limitations.

Theoretical Background 2

2.1 Corporate Financing

Corporate financing is a critical element in the business world. It influences strategic decision making and facilitates the implementation of operational and growth initiatives. More than just a facet of financial management, it acts as a key driver and supporter of diverse business activities. This section ventures into the domain of corporate finance, commencing with an exploration of its two principal methods: equity and debt financing. These two avenues, which each have unique traits and implications, are integral to forming a company's financial structure and strategic options.

Central to the discussion is an in-depth analysis of corporate bonds, which is a predominant form of debt financing. This chapter aims to unravel the complexities of corporate bonds, covering their entire lifecycle and the intricate mechanisms that govern their pricing. This detailed examination sets the stage for a thorough assessment evaluating how blockchain technology could redefine traditional practices in corporate bond issuance and trading, thereby reshaping the broader landscape of corporate financing.

2.1.1 Equity Versus Debt Financing

In the realm of corporate financing, companies often face pivotal decisions on how to optimally secure funds essential for both their operations and future growth. Central to these decisions is the choice between two predominant avenues: equity and debt financing.

M. M. Grossmann, *Blockchain-Based Bonds*, BestMasters,
https://doi.org/10.1007/978-3-658-45311-4_2

Equity financing involves raising capital by issuing company shares, a process that can lead to ownership dilution and altered control dynamics. Conversely, debt financing, through means such as bank loans or bonds, allows companies to raise funds in a way that does not affect ownership, although it carries interest commitments and default risks (Myers, 2001). Theoretical models like the one described by Modigliani and Miller (1958) propose that, in a perfect market that is devoid of taxes, bankruptcy costs, and other imperfections, a firm's capital structure—whether it relies on debt or equity—should neither influence its value nor the cost or the availability of capital.

However, this principle does not hold true in practice, which is why the optimal choice of capital structure remains a debated topic in academic circles (Myers, 2001). Diverse theories provide varying viewpoints, such as the trade-off theory, which advocates for debt issuance to leverage tax benefits (Kraus & Litzenberger, 1973), the pecking order theory, which favors equity financing to reduce information asymmetry (Myers & Majluf, 1984), or the market timing theory, which posits that firms adjust their capital structure based on equity market conditions (Baker & Wurgler, 2002).

Beyond theoretical models, the practical side of the capital structure choice involves selecting from a broad spectrum of financing instruments. Companies can choose from various equity financing options—like common and preferred stocks—and debt financing alternatives, including corporate bonds, bank loans, and commercial papers. Additionally, hybrid instruments, such as convertible bonds, combine features of both equity and debt. However, this paper will focus specifically on one such instrument: corporate bonds.

2.1.2 Corporate Bonds

Corporate bonds are debt securities issued by companies, primarily for the purpose of re-financing (Bessembinder & Maxwell, 2008). However, the proceeds from corporate bonds can also be used for other specific purposes, such as acquisitions or investments (Celik et al., 2015). The global corporate bond market is huge: It encompassed a global volume of non-financial and financial corporate debt of over €23 trillion at the end of the third quarter 2023 (BIS, 2023).

Bonds represent a promise by the issuing company to repay the principal amount at maturity, and they usually pay bondholders a specified amount of interest over a predetermined period of time (Mukherjee, 2012). Primary ways of categorizing corporate bonds include differentiating according to their maturities or their interest-rate structures. According to the United States Securities and

Exchange Commission, maturities range from short-term (up to three years), and medium-term (four to ten years), to long-term (above 10 years; SEC, 2013).

From an interest-rate perspective, market players mainly distinguish between fixed-rate bonds, floating-rate bonds, and zero-coupon bonds (Chen, 2022). According to Mukherjee (2012), they can be characterized as follows: While fixed-rate bonds, which are the most common type, pay a consistent coupon throughout their life with the principal returned at maturity, floating rate bonds differ in that their coupon rate is not constant and is adjusted in pre-defined time intervals. Conversely, zero-coupon bonds are issued at a discount to their face value and mature at par. The difference between the purchase price and the face value effectively serves as the interest, accruing over the bond's lifespan, under the assumption of a prevailing positive interest-rate environment.

One of the primary benefits for corporations issuing bonds is the ability to secure large amounts of capital at longer maturities. Having this ability is especially favorable in times of low interest rates (Celik et al., 2015). Moreover, issuing bonds allows companies to diversify their sources of financing, which in turn reduces their reliance on other funding channels, like bank loans (Santos, 2010).

2.1.2.1 Lifecycle

A corporate bond requires close collaboration among diverse stakeholders throughout its whole lifecycle. This section will provide a foundational understanding of the process, which is depicted in Fig. 2.1. However, the specifics may vary depending on jurisdictional requirements and company-specific protocols and, therefore, might require close legal support.

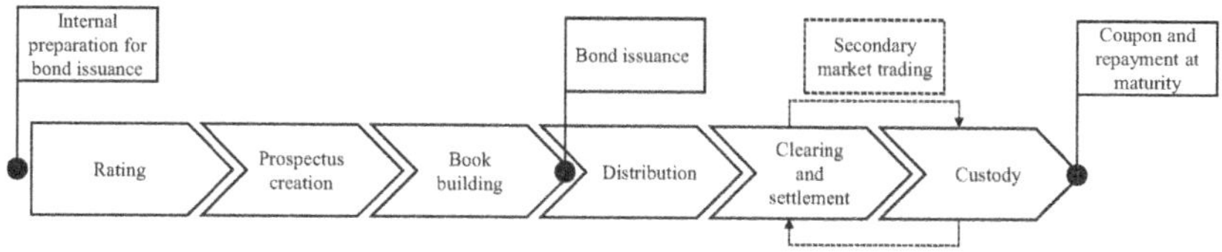

Fig. 2.1 Corporate-Bond Lifecycle. (Source: Own illustration)

Before embarking on a bond issuance, the issuing company, as well as the bond to be issued, usually receive a rating from an agency such as Moody's, Standard & Poor's, or Fitch, which assesses the company's creditworthiness. These ratings have the potential to substantially influence investor decisions and lending terms. It is noteworthy that the ratings for individual bonds can differ. Occasionally, they surpass or fall below the primary issuer rating, e.g., depending on the bond's priority (May, 2010). Altman et al. (2004) demonstrate that higher credit ratings correlate with greater recovery rates and lower default risks.

Bond ratings can generally be divided into two categories: "investment grade," indicating lower credit risk, and "speculative grade," denoting a significantly higher default risk. Standard & Poor's, for instance, considers all ratings from AAA to BBB– "investment grade" and BB+to D "speculative grade" (S&P, 2022). Bessembinder and Maxwell (2008) highlight that regulated financial entities usually have stricter rules regarding non-investment-grade bonds, and some institutions, like pension funds, are even limited in how much of this type of debt they can hold.

After obtaining a rating, the company drafts the bond prospectus. This document is legally mandated for protecting investor interests. It provides a detailed view on the bond offering and the issuer. This view includes the company's financial health, how it plans to use the funds raised, and key details of the bond, which encompass the bond's rating, maturity date, interest rate, and other relevant terms. While this requirement is generally applicable, there are exceptions based on specific conditions. These conditions might involve the qualification level of the targeted investors or the denomination of the bond. For instance, the disclosure requirements are less stringent when the bond is only to be made available to institutional investors, who are deemed to have a broader understanding and greater capability to assess risks compared to retail investors (EU, 2017).

In line with these regulations, companies can establish debt issuance programs governed by a single prospectus. This option requires quarterly updates and annual approval from the relevant national authority. In Germany, responsibility for such approvals falls to the Federal Financial Supervisory Authority *("Bundesanstalt fuer Finanzdienstleistungsaufsicht"),* commonly known as *"BaFin"* (BaFin, 2023a). This approach facilitates multiple bond issuances within a single year, thereby streamlining the process and minimizing the need for frequent approvals and administrative work.

In the next phase, issuers collaborate with one or more investment banks to identify potential investors and finalize the bond details. Typically, the focus is on institutional investors, such as banks and insurance companies, as they usually buy large volumes (Nikolova et al., 2020) and apply for the already outlined reduced disclosure requirements for issuers (EU, 2017). This tendency is also observed by Celik et al. (2015), who observed that the ownership of corporate bonds predominantly lies with institutional entities, with only a minor portion held by retail investors.

After finalizing its features, the bond is prepared for issuance in the primary market. It is important to note that the issuance can be paused at any point before release, particularly if significant changes occur in financial or economic conditions (Takaoka & Takahashi, 2022).

The bank initially provides interested parties with an overview of the issuance, conducts due diligence calls, and engages in book building to gauge initial investment interest. Such data is vital for discerning market preferences and, if needed, for adjusting the bond's price or yield to align supply with demand (Nikolova et al., 2020). Drawing from Bord and Santos (2012), the bank's role in distributing the bonds to investors can vary. It may either underwrite the issue, purchasing bonds from the issuer to sell to investors, or operate on a best-effort basis, coordinating direct sales from the issuer to investors without guaranteeing the placement of the entire amount.

Post-issuance—from primary market distribution to secondary-market trading and all the way to repayment at maturity—financial market infrastructure (FMI) providers play a crucial role. FMIs underpin the smooth functioning of financial markets by facilitating transactions, ensuring safekeeping of assets, and promoting stability and efficiency (RBA, 2023). After the financial crisis in 2007/2008, governance by law increased significantly (Goldberg & Nozawa, 2021). Within this setting, the regulator designated FMIs a vital function in fortifying financial markets following the turmoil (Saguato, 2017). Their tasks are essentially divided between two relevant providers: clearinghouses and central securities depositories.

"Clearing refers to everything prior to settlement, establishing who owes what to whom and when" (Milne, 2016, p. 335). In this context, a clearinghouse acts as an intermediary in post-trade financial activities, ensuring contract fulfillment even if a party defaults. By serving as a central counterparty (CCP), it buys from every seller and sells to every buyer. This role not only guarantees contract completion but also positions the clearinghouse as a key risk mitigator. In the event of a member's default, it methodically disperses the ensuing losses among its solvent members, thereby safeguarding broader market stability (Saguato, 2017).

Central securities depositories (CSDs) primarily handle the documentation of securities ("notary service"), maintain top-level securities accounts ("central maintenance service" or "top-tier safekeeping") and typically oversee the settlement process, particularly the monetary aspect of securities trading transactions. As such, they handle domestic and international securities settlements, facilitate timely bond payments and maturity returns, enforce bond terms, and ease issuer-investor communications. CSDs centralize operations with direct connections to all involved parties and safeguard the (physical) bond's certificate, which represents its total value (Nougayrede, 2018).

According to EU Regulation 909/2014, Article 3(2), all securities that are listed or traded on an exchange must be registered with a CSD (EU, 2014b). Although not access restricted, the CSD market is organized in a very monopolistic way, for example with Clearstream covering the German and Luxembourg market (Clearstream, 2019). According to Nougayrede (2018), other major global players, besides Clearstream, are Euroclear and DTC. Together, the three cover a significant share of the global securities market.

To summarize the roles of clearinghouses and CSDs: While clearinghouses ensure that the trade *can* happen by managing risks and interposing itself, CSDs make sure that the trade *does* happen by managing the final exchange and storage of assets, as illustrated in Fig. 2.2.

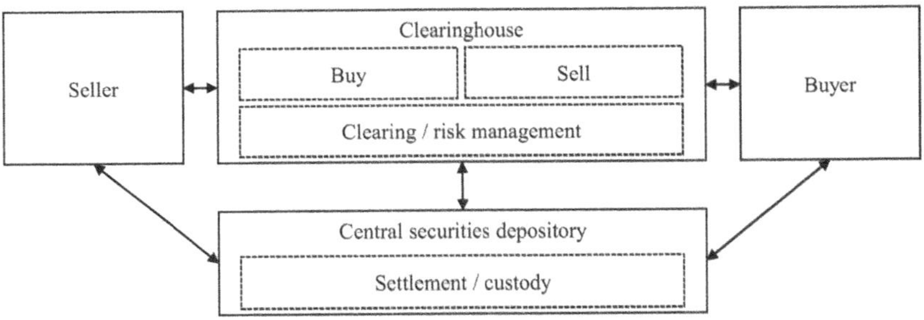

Fig. 2.2 Role of Clearinghouses and CSDs. (Source: Own illustration)

In a nutshell, the lifecycle of a corporate bond involves several key phases. Initially, independent agencies conduct a creditworthiness evaluation. Following this assessment, the bond prospectus is drafted, paving the way for the bond's market introduction. Issuers then team up with investment banks that gauge investor interest and facilitate the bond's distribution at issuance. Post-issuance, clearinghouses are responsible for managing trade-related risks and ensuring transactions are completed efficiently. Concurrently, CSDs handle the intricate tasks of documentation, maintenance, and settlement of the bond, including overseeing the distribution of coupon payments and managing the bond at maturity. All of this is meant to contribute to ensuring financial market stability and efficiency.

2.1.2.2 Pricing

The pricing of corporate bonds is fundamentally anchored in their yield, which is the total annual return an investor expects when holding a bond to a given maturity. The yield comprises the risk-free rate, typically determined by a government bond with the same maturity, and the credit spread, which compensates investors for the additional risks of holding a corporate bond compared to its risk-free alternative (Amato & Remolona, 2003). However, the precise makeup of the credit spread remains a topic of contention in academic circles, frequently referred to as the "credit spread puzzle" (Christensen, 2008). Instead of joining the debate, this paper will spotlight some major drivers of the spread.

Broader economic developments not only influence central bank decisions, and thus implicitly the risk-free rate, but also corporate spreads: As outlined by Mokdadi and Saadaoui (2023), geopolitical risks can cause volatility in commodity prices, leading to economic shocks and higher inflation rates in importing countries. These effects also raise business risks that increase the probability of default and hence corporate bond spreads. Huang et al. (2019) emphasize that exchange rate fluctuations also impact corporate bond spreads. Referring to the example of a Chinese company, they show that appreciation of the Chinese currency Renminbi against the U.S. dollar reduces corporate risk of local companies, and therefore credit spreads, and vice versa.

The question of whether industry risks also affect corporate bond spreads is controversial. While Durbin and Ng (2005) highlight that, for emerging markets, the explanatory power of industry effects is not significant with respect to spreads, Garay et al. (2019) find a significant correlation in their sample for the basic materials, energy, communications and technology industries. They also show that, in some countries, the "sovereign ceiling" rule is violated. This rule states that a private entity's credit rating cannot exceed its home country's sovereign rating. However, adherence to this policy by credit agencies has become more flexible since the late 1990s (Huang & Shen, 2015).

Gabbi and Sironi (2005) state that the financial health and credit rating of the bond issuer are primary determinants of the spread. They outline that bonds from issuers with high credit ratings usually command lower spreads, reflecting their smaller perceived risk. As Guedes and Pinto (2023) observed, however, if there are more ratings available, consistency throughout the ratings plays a crucial role. They find that, when there are discrepancies in ratings from multiple agencies, investors often demand an additional risk premium.

A bond's liquidity, which is the ease with which it can be traded, also affects its spread. Bonds that are less frequently traded or are perceived as less liquid generally have higher spreads due to the associated trading challenges (Kempf &

Uhrig-Homburg, 2000). Liquidity is vital for investors as it provides the flexibility to respond to market changes and is crucial for effective risk management, allowing timely exits from positions in adverse conditions (Bao et al., 2011). This assessment is in line with De Jong and Driessen (2006), who observed that a significant portion of the credit spread can be attributed to liquidity. The steadier the balance of demand and supply for transactions on the secondary market, the better its liquidity and the lower the spread.

Bao et al. (2011) show that liquidity tends to decline as the bond ages and gets closer to maturity but positively correlates with the size of its issuance. Additionally, unforeseen global events, such as the COVID-19 pandemic, can heighten investor uncertainty and further deteriorate liquidity, a phenomenon observed by O'Hara and Zhou (2021).

According to Cai et al. (2007), bonds with smaller issuance sizes often see limited post-issuance trading on secondary markets, as they are typically acquired by just a few institutional investors. Another factor to consider is market reach: global bonds, which are issued across various countries and currencies, naturally possess greater liquidity than bonds limited to just one market (Petrasek, 2012). Liquidity in the secondary market is essential for determining prices for primary issuances: As Mukherjee (2012) notes, an illiquid market can obstruct the proper pricing of corporate bonds. Low trading volume and a high bid-ask spread usually indicate illiquidity (Loncarski & Szilagyi, 2012).

In conclusion, the pricing of corporate bonds is a multifaceted process that is rooted in its yield, although the exact components of the credit spread remain debated. This chapter has illuminated some of the primary drivers of the spread, emphasizing the intricate interplay of geopolitical risks, industry effects, issuer credit ratings, and liquidity dynamics in shaping bond pricing.

2.2 Blockchain Technology

The following chapter delves into blockchain technology to explain the aspects that are essential for understanding and assessing its potential to revolutionize the corporate bond market. As a relatively recent and complex innovation, blockchain remains an enigma to many in the field of corporate finance. Hence, this section is designed to demystify the technology and offer a detailed foundation in its core principles, functionalities, and associated challenges. It ensures that readers—regardless of their familiarity with the technology—are well-equipped to engage with the potential of blockchain in corporate finance.

2.2.1 Basic Principles

A blockchain, at its simplest, is a decentralized, transparent, and secure digital ledger system where information is stored in cryptographically interconnected blocks across multiple computers (nodes), making the data highly resistant to retroactive modification or manipulation (Efanov & Roschin, 2018). Even if the terms "distributed ledger technology," or "DLT," and "blockchain" are often used interchangeably in academic literature, subtle differences exist between the two: DLT broadly refers to any decentralized digital system that records transactions across multiple sites without a central authority. In contrast, blockchain is a specific kind of DLT that stores data in interconnected blocks (Bruehl, 2017).

Blockchain technology has the potential to disrupt entire sectors, a point highlighted by Oh and Shong (2017). Crosby et al. (2016) even suggest that blockchain could become "the new engine of growth in [the] digital economy" (p. 9). Gaur (2020) emphasizes the significance of this technology, stating that it "has the promise to change the world (once again) as we know it" (p. 1).

Its origin is embedded in the early 1990s, when Stuart Haber and W. Scott Stornetta proposed an archetypal form of this technology, detailing the structure of what they termed a "chain of timestamps" (Haber & Stornetta, 1991, p. 104). Their innovation was a system designed for timestamping digital documents in a way that made it impossible to backdate or alter the timestamps. This advancement was pivotal in the evolution of blockchain technology, as it introduced the concept of a cryptographically secure chain of blocks. However, this early version lacked the decentralized, peer-to-peer (P2P) characteristics that define modern blockchain systems.

Building on this work, Nakamoto (2008) proposed the electronic cash system "Bitcoin." Adding a decentralized consensus mechanism, they proposed the first practical solution allowing for P2P transactions while successfully circumventing the problem of double-spending of digital tokens without a trusted intermediary (Pass et al., 2017). Implemented in 2009 by establishing the first block in the chain, the so-called "genesis block," it marked the inception of contemporary blockchains (Crosby et al., 2016).

As outlined by Tapscott and Tapscott (2017), blockchains are unique as they can be characterized by the following key features:

(1) **Distributed database:** In a blockchain system, every participant maintains a current version of the entire database along with its comprehensive transaction history. This architecture significantly hinders deletion, tampering, or revision of the data (Iansiti & Lakhani, 2017). Thus, each participant can

directly verify the records of their transaction partners without intermediaries (Tapscott & Tapscott, 2017). As the blockchain operates as a decentralized digital ledger storing "all transactions or digital events that have been executed and shared among participating parties" (Crosby et al., 2016, p. 7), no entity possesses single control over the data or information (Tapscott & Tapscott, 2017).

(2) **Peer-to-peer transmission:** Blockchain employs a P2P model facilitating direct communication between peers (Tapscott & Tapscott, 2017). This communication takes place nearly in real time. As a result, transactions can be settled instantly (Hofmann et al., 2018). By each node storing and forwarding information to all other nodes in the network, blockchain technology enables reliable and auditable interactions in a trustless environment (Christidis & Devetsikiotis, 2016). Hence, there is no need for a central administrator (Oh & Shong, 2017).

(3) **Transparency with pseudonymity:** Despite the high level of transparency, where every transaction and its value are accessible to anyone within the system, the users' identities can remain concealed (Iansiti & Lakhani, 2017). Each user or node in the blockchain is assigned a unique alphanumeric address, which is called a "public key" (Tapscott & Tapscott, 2017). It is available to everyone and allows transactions to be identified unambiguously without disclosing the true identity of the parties involved in the transaction (Abou Jaoude & Saade, 2019).

"This is similar to the level of information released by stock exchanges, where the time and size of individual trades, the 'tape', is made public, but without telling who the parties were" (Nakamoto, 2008, p. 6). Fraudulent action through the knowledge of a public key, e.g., performing transactions on behalf of another party, is not possible. An additional private key, which is strictly known by the individual only, is required to authorize transactions (Abou Jaoude & Saade, 2019).

(4) **Irreversibility of records:** Due to the blockchain's structural design, once a transaction is logged and accepted, the records become immutable (Agbo et al., 2019). They are intrinsically linked to every transaction record preceding them, resulting in an irreversible chain (Nakamoto, 2008). This immutability is ensured through the deployment of various computational algorithms and methods that guarantee the permanence of records, their chronological order, and their availability to all network participants (Tapscott & Tapscott, 2017). By leveraging this feature, Nakamoto (2008) ensured that, in their Bitcoin network, the same digital token could not be spent more than once.

(5) **Computational logic:** As blockchain transactions are digital, they can be tied to computational logic, meaning that they can be programmed (Tapscott & Tapscott, 2017). This feature allows the creation of "smart contracts." In essence, they are computer programs that automatically enforce the terms of a contract when coded conditions are met (Yli-Huumo et al., 2016). This approach offers a novel level of automation and efficiency by lessening bureaucratic processes and simplifying multi-step procedures (Abou Jaoude & Saade, 2019).

2.2.2 Creating Records on Blockchains

Recording a transaction on a blockchain entails a series of operations involving digital signatures, cryptographic hashing and consensus algorithms, each of which is crucial to the integrity and security of the system (Nakamoto, 2008). The following sections will describe how a transaction is inscribed onto a blockchain.

2.2.2.1 Transaction Creation and Validation

The process begins when a user initiates a transaction, which could involve transferring cryptocurrency, executing a smart contract, or tasking any other action that changes the state of the blockchain (Li & Palanisamy, 2020). As outlined, each network participant possesses a public-private key pair, with the public key acting as the user's address and the private key as a means for authentication (Baucas et al., 2021). A transaction incorporates the initiator's public key, the recipient's public key, and the transaction message, which encapsulates all the necessary details and instructions on the processing actions (Agbo et al., 2019). Bundled together, the data is cryptographically signed with the user's private key and broadcasted to the network for execution (Nakamoto, 2008).

All nodes within the system are promptly notified of the transactional activity; however, as long as the transaction has not yet been validated by the community, it remains unconfirmed (Levis et al., 2021). During the validation phase, nodes across the network assess transactions, e.g., for syntactical integrity, signature authenticity, or sufficient balance in the case of a transfer (Crosby et al., 2016). Once verified, these transactions are temporarily stored in the designated repository of each node, which is commonly referred to as "memory pool" or "mem-pool." There, they wait to be integrated into a block (Kasahara, 2021). Fig. 2.3 visualizes this process.

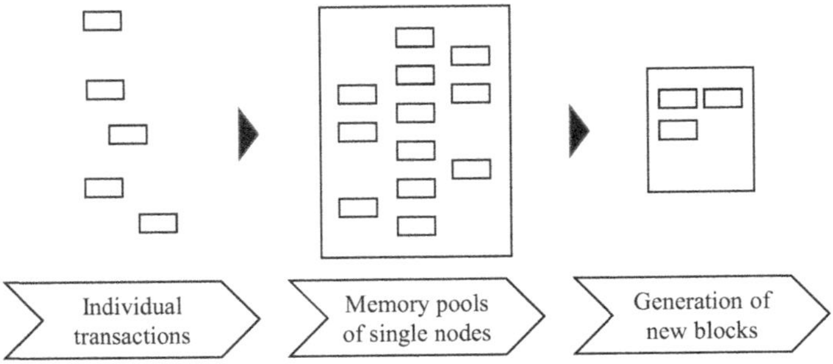

Fig. 2.3 Transaction Processing in Blockchains. (Source: Own illustration)

2.2.2.2 Block Creation and Integration into the Blockchain

Generally, a "block" is a set of various validated transactions that are periodically grouped together (Sguanci et al., 2021). Every block contains a unique code, known as the "hash." The hash is derived by processing the details of the transactions inside the block through a cryptographic function, resulting in a fixed-size string of characters that appears to be random (Abou Jaoude & Saade, 2019). Crosby et al. (2016) compare the hash to a "fingerprint" (p. 15), as by definition no two distinct transactions will yield identical hash results (Haber & Stornetta, 1991).

Importantly, when a block is added, it also references the hash of the preceding block (Nofer et al., 2017). Thus, a linked chain of blocks is created, which is why it is termed a "blockchain" (Meiklejohn et al., 2016). If any information within a block is modified, its hash will inevitably change (Cocco & Marchesi, 2016). Since the subsequent block's reference to the previous hash will remain unchanged, potential tampering would be signaled instantly (Kasahara, 2021). A simplified outline of a blockchain's fundamental concept is shown in Fig. 2.4.

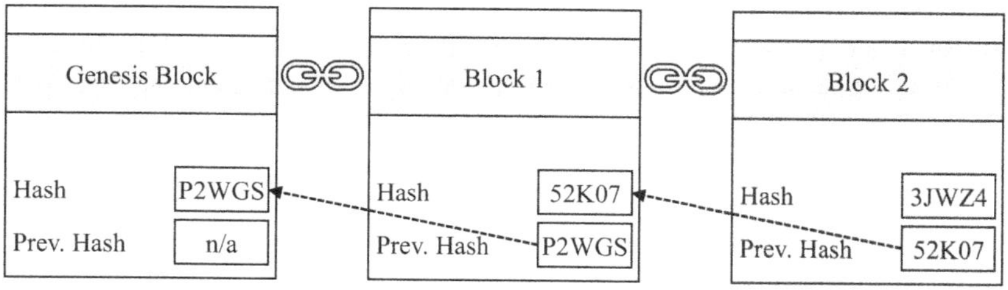

Fig. 2.4 Simplified Outline of a Blockchain. (Source: Own illustration)

2.2.3 Consensus Algorithms

The consensus mechanism, a core component of a blockchain's architecture, determines how participants agree on adding new blocks. This algorithm is crucial for a blockchain's functionality and security and ensures unanimous agreement on transaction validity. This agreement is essential to prevent fraud and maintain the integrity of the data stored on the blockchain (Weerawarna et al., 2023).

Lashkari and Musilek (2021) acknowledge a range of consensus mechanisms, with proof of work (PoW) and proof of stake (PoS) being the most notable, as highlighted by Yan (2022). Hence, this section will concentrate on the block creation and integration processes with these two mechanisms. For this purpose, Bitcoin and Ethereum—the best-known blockchain networks according to Michael and Pratt (2023)—will be used as case studies to elucidate the process of achieving consensus in PoW and PoS systems respectively. However, due to the use of specific examples, it is important to note that the findings may not be entirely applicable to other blockchain systems, even if they also rely on PoW or PoS.

2.2.3.1 Proof of Work

The PoW consensus process initiates with miners grouping transactions from their mem-pool to compile a block, as documented by Meiklejohn et al. (2016). On the Bitcoin blockchain, the standard block size is capped at one megabyte (MB), which accommodates approximately 2,759 transactions based on an average transaction size of 380 bytes (Sguanci et al., 2021). The block-size limitation is intended to allow for swift distribution across the network, which is a design choice aimed at network efficiency (Croman et al., 2016).

The present study acknowledges the Segregated Witness (SegWit) update to Bitcoin in 2017 without providing an in-depth analysis. SegWit has facilitated an increase in the block's transaction capacity by segregating the signature data and introducing a new block-weight metric. This innovation allows for effectively accommodating more than the standard 2,759 transactions, a change that could result in blocks exceeding the original 1 MB base block size (Perez-Sola et al., 2019).

Miners may freely choose from all valid transactions in their mem-pool when assembling a block. Consequently, users usually offer a transaction fee to guarantee the inclusion of their transactions in the blockchain (Nakamoto, 2008). According to Gebraselase et al. (2021) and Lavi et al. (2022), miners are inclined to prioritize transactions that offer higher fees. As a result, transaction fees emerge as an effective incentive for accelerating the inclusion of a transaction in the blockchain.

Once a block is formed, a mathematical puzzle, the "proof of work," related to the block's content is presented to the respective miner (Bonneau et al., 2015). The challenge entails identifying a particular input termed a "nonce." The nonce—together with the transactions of the current block and the hash of the previous block—must generate an output that starts with a predetermined number of zeros when inserted into a hash function (Crosby et al., 2016). Using their computational power, miners across the network try to solve the puzzle for their respective block at the same time (Khan et al., 2021).

The first miner who has successfully solved its puzzle broadcasts its block to the network for verification. If the proposed answer is correct, the new block containing the grouped transactions is added to the blockchain. The miner who successfully adds this block is compensated in two ways: They receive a "block reward" consisting of newly minted Bitcoins, and they collect the fees associated with the transactions included in the block (Nakamoto, 2008). Miners are motivated to focus only on legitimate blocks: Since the network rejects invalid blocks, they would not receive any rewards for working on them (Bonneau et al., 2015).

The initial block reward, as outlined by Cocco and Marchesi (2016), was set at 50 Bitcoins (BTC) and was designed to halve after every 210,000 blocks, a scenario that typically occurs around every four years. Since the last halving in April 2024, the mining reward per block has been 3.125 BTC. Consequently, this halving process will continue until around 2140, after which no new bitcoins will be minted (Abrol, 2023). As the block reward diminishes over time, transaction fees will progressively become the primary incentive for miners to participate in the network (Lavi et al., 2022). This development is in line with Moeser and Boehme (2015), who assume that this situation will be reflected in rising transaction fees.

Systematically adjusting the intricacy of the computational challenge ensures that, in the Bitcoin network, the resolution process takes around ten minutes on average (Crosby et al., 2016). This design choice allows nodes ample time for consensus (Bonneau et al., 2015) and for data dissemination throughout the network (Sompolinsky & Zohar, 2015).

If two valid solutions are found nearly simultaneously, a temporary fork occurs (Christidis & Devetsikiotis, 2016). Different parts of the network validate and build upon the block they receive first, possibly containing vastly distinct or conflicting transactions (Wood, 2014). This situation leads to two competing chains with miners each working on their version of the chain (Bonneau et al., 2015).

The protocol typically favors the chain with the most accumulated proof of work, a preference that is often referred to as the "longest chain rule:" When one chain gets extended, making it longer than the other, the network converges on that chain, and the shorter chain is discarded (Christidis & Devetsikiotis, 2016). Consequently, any unique transactions from the discarded block are revoked, which underscores the importance of waiting for multiple confirmations to ensure a transaction's finality. From a practical client view, it has proven to be worthwhile to wait six additional confirmation blocks before finally accepting that a transaction was published (Bonneau et al., 2015).

Owing to their robust architecture, PoW blockchains boast security and integrity. However, it is also necessary to recognize the associated challenges and downsides: To enhance their chances of creating blocks and earning rewards, miners can collaborate in so-called "mining pools" to combine their computational resources (Kasahara, 2021). Such collaboration can lead to centralization, especially if a few dominant pools control a significant portion of the network's power (Buterin, 2014). This concentration raises the risk of a so-called "51% attack," in which an entity with majority control could manipulate transaction history and, for instance, double-spend coins (Efanov & Roschin, 2018).

Yet, to successfully disguise the alteration, it would be necessary to recompute the PoW for the modified block and all subsequent blocks (Nakamoto, 2008). For this reason, a potential attacker would need immense computational power and energy (Lin, 2023). Moreover, it would essentially harm its own interests, as a successful assault would erode confidence in the network and lower the cryptocurrency's value (Larimer, 2013).

However, Kroll et al. (2013) point out, that theoretically, this downside does not necessarily counter the potential benefits of such attacks: For one thing, parties with short positions in the network's foundational cryptocurrencies might stand to gain from the subsequent price decline. In addition, there might be attackers who want to disrupt or destroy the network without a direct financial benefit because they are motivated by non-economic factors, for instance to express social protest (Becker et al., 2013).

While recognized and understood, this paper will not delve deeper into the details of 51% attacks and other types of blockchain attacks. They are multifaceted and include, among others, "Sybil attacks," in which adversaries create multiple virtual nodes to manipulate and disrupt the network's operations (Swathi et al., 2019) and block-withholding attacks, in which malicious miners withhold block solutions to undermine the rewards of honest participants (Tosh et al., 2017).

However, as highlighted by Aggarwal and Kumar (2021), numerous strategies and solutions have already been proposed to counteract the risks of these attacks, e.g., by Soska et al. (2016), who propose a decentralized marketplace resistant against Sybil attacks, or Mihaljevic et al. (2022), who introduce a pool-mining method using symmetric encryption to counteract block withholding.

Another challenge of PoW blockchains is their limited transaction throughput. Due to this limitation, Bitcoin can process only around seven transactions per second (Nguyen et al., 2019), which poses challenges with regard to scalability (Vukolic, 2016). This shortcoming is especially pronounced when compared to traditional transaction systems like Visa or PayPal, which are capable of processing 1,700 and 193 transactions per second respectively (Hafid et al., 2020). This limitation is directly linked to Bitcoin's emphasis on security and decentralization: As highlighted before, the capped block size promotes rapid network transmission, and with block intervals set to roughly 10 minutes, it is ensured that nodes can effectively achieve consensus.

Lastly, another major challenge and point of criticism of PoW blockchains is the energy-intensive mining process (Dominguez Anguiano & Parte, 2023; Y. Zhou et al., 2020). To make the Bitcoin network's energy consumption tangible, Kohli et al. (2023) refer to energy-tracking studies such as Digiconomist and the Cambridge Bitcoin Energy Consumption Index (CBECI), which are keeping a running estimate: As of January 12, 2024, the estimated energy consumption of the Bitcoin network is 137.7 TWh per year. This level of energy usage is comparable to the annual consumption of countries like Ukraine and Malaysia, hypothetically ranking 27th in a global country comparison, and raises significant sustainability concerns (Cocco et al., 2017).

As such, it can be concluded that PoW provides a robust foundation for blockchain consensus. However, balancing its strengths in security and integrity with challenges in centralization, scalability, and energy consumption remain a pivotal concern for further adoption.

2.2.3.2 Proof of Stake

The PoS consensus mechanism was developed primarily to mitigate the substantial energy consumption and associated environmental concerns of PoW blockchains (Gazi et al., 2018). Additionally, it addresses centralization issues that arise when a few large mining pools dominate the network. PoS aims to efficiently reach consensus while maintaining the blockchain's security and decentralization, thus preserving its integrity without the extensive energy requirements of PoW systems (Ethereum, 2023e).

The Ethereum network, which had previously relied on a PoW consensus mechanism, transitioned to Ethereum 2.0 and adopted a PoS approach. This shift was marked by "The Merge" in September 2022, which integrated the new PoS-based "Beacon Chain" with the original PoW-based Ethereum Mainnet (Ethereum, 2023b). Initial empirical research by Kapengut and Mizrach (2023) indicates that this transition resulted in a substantial 99.9% reduction in energy consumption, making Ethereum more environmentally-friendly. In addition, this reduction came along with a 19% decrease in network concentration, enhancing network security (Uzsoki, 2019). It also laid the groundwork for future scalability improvements that are currently in development (Ethereum, 2023b).

In blockchain networks that employ PoS rather than PoW, participants known as "validators" play a role akin to miners (Kapengut & Mizrach, 2023). Unlike the computation-intensive process of mining in PoW, PoS operates on the principle of choosing validators based on their willingness to stake a certain amount of the network's cryptocurrency as collateral (Nguyen et al., 2019). Moreover, other networks, like Peercoin, utilize additional criteria to determine a stake's eligibility for validator qualification. One such criterion may be "coin age," which refers to the ownership duration of the pledged coins (King & Nadal, 2012).

However, to participate in Ethereum's PoS system as a validator, a node only needs to stake 32 Ether (ETH). Once staked, the node becomes part of the consensus process, participating in block validation and creation. Validators for proposing and validating new blocks are selected pseudo-randomly at regular intervals. In the system, time is organized into "epochs," which are each divided into 32 slots of 12 seconds. In each epoch, different validators are chosen to propose blocks, and committees are formed to vote on their validity. This system ensures that all validators have the opportunity to contribute to network maintenance by validating and proposing blocks over time, though not necessarily in every slot (Ethereum, 2023c).

Regular rotation of validators in the system prevents any single validator from monopolizing the block creation process, thereby promoting decentralization. Moreover, this approach greatly reduces energy consumption by eliminating the need for nodes to solve complex puzzles to propose new blocks, making the process more environmentally sustainable, as noted by Cortes-Goicoechea et al. (2023).

At the beginning of each epoch within the Ethereum PoS system, validator attestations collectively establish the blockchain's state. If consensus is achieved, with at least two-thirds of the total staked ETH concurring, this state is recognized as a "justified checkpoint." This verification step is repeated at the start of every epoch. When a subsequent epoch also attains a "supermajority" consensus (two-thirds) at its beginning, a "supermajority link" is formed between these checkpoints. As a result, the blocks prior to the earlier checkpoint are considered "finalized," making them an immutable part of the blockchain's history. This state of finality is critical as it denotes that these blocks cannot be changed without incurring significant penalties under the network's established consensus rules (Ethereum, 2023c).

If validators fail to achieve consensus regarding the blockchain's state, possibly due to network delays, temporary forks may occur (Buterin & Griffith, 2017). In traditional PoS systems, this divergence can be exploited due to the "nothing at stake" problem: Since validators in PoS do not expend significant resources like they do in PoW systems, they could be inclined to support multiple forks at once, undermining the networks' security and consensus (Wang et al., 2019).

To counter the "nothing at stake" problem, Ethereum relies on penalties or "slashing" (Ethereum, 2023d). If validators act maliciously or fail to properly validate, for instance because of being offline, they can lose a portion or all of their staked coins (Kapengut & Mizrach, 2023). However, Saleh (2021) argues that implementing a minimum stake threshold for being eligible to update the blockchain, or offering sufficiently low block rewards—which would remove the only potential gain from propagating disagreement—could tackle the problem in the same way: Both approaches would make fraudulent behavior unattractive, because perpetuating discrepancies in the blockchain could devalue the underlying coin, directly impacting the validator's wealth. To reunify the network after a fork, Ethereum prioritizes the chain that has the greatest consensus among validators on the most recent blocks (Buterin et al., 2020).

PoS networks are inherently more complex than PoW networks, leading to a broader spectrum of potential security threats. For example, the risk of a 51% attack persists in PoS. However, such an attack might be more challenging and riskier because a majority of the staked currency must be owned. Ethereum's PoS is fortified with protocol-level defenses like the "finality gadget," which prevents finalized blocks from being altered. As indicated, this paper will not explore various types of blockchain attacks in depth, nor will it offer a comparative analysis of the security of PoW versus PoS (Ethereum, 2023c).

To execute a transaction on the Ethereum network, users pay a "gas fee" that consists of a variable base fee, which is adjusted in accordance with network demand, and an optional tip for faster transaction processing. The base fee is not paid to the validators, but is burned, reducing ETH's circulating supply and indirectly rewarding holders by exerting a deflationary effect (Roughgarden, 2020).

Similar to Bitcoin, Ethereum's validator compensation system encourages active and honest participation (Cortes-Goicoechea et al., 2023). This system includes rewards for validators, which are structured around two main components: proposer rewards for including valid attestations in their block and attester rewards for attesting to the correct block. Both types of rewards are funded by the issuance of new ETH. In addition, block proposers receive the tips that users pay for faster transaction processing (Buterin et al., 2020).

In conclusion, PoS effectively tackles key issues of PoW, such as high energy consumption and network centralization. However, PoS introduces its own complexities, including potentially increased vulnerability to attacks. Scalability challenges persist, yet the foundation for future enhancements has been established. Ethereum's transition to PoS marks a significant milestone in blockchain development, while still emphasizing the need for continuous development to overcome remaining challenges.

2.2.4 Scalability Trilemma

Achieving high transaction rates per second without compromising system security or decentralization is a challenge that has been formalized as the "scalability trilemma" (Q. Zhou et al., 2020). Typically, enhancing one of these attributes negatively impacts at least one of the others, leading to complex trade-offs (see Fig. 2.5). As this trilemma has not been resolved yet, approaches to date have tended to focus on finding the most advantageous position in the trade-off (Sguanci et al., 2021).

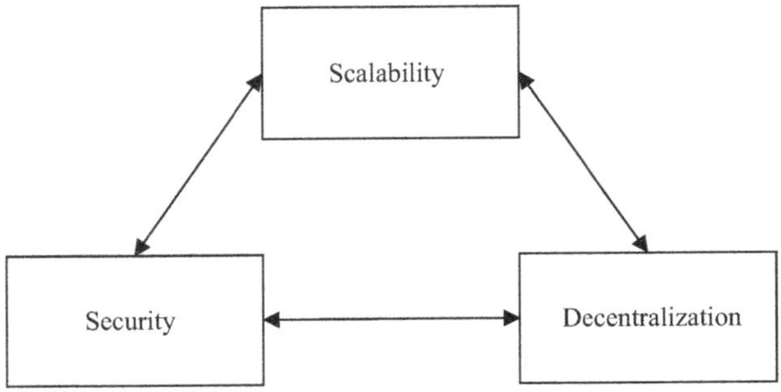

Fig. 2.5 Scalability Trilemma of Blockchains. (Source: Adapted from Hafid et al. (2020), p. 1)

Existing approaches to increasing transaction rates per second—a prerequisite for scalability—have concentrated on so-called Layer-1 and Layer-2 solutions (Hafid et al., 2020).

Layer-1 solutions involve altering blockchain fundamentals, such as introducing new consensus mechanisms, reducing transaction-confirmation times, or increasing block sizes (Gangwal et al., 2023). However, while reduced latency leads to elevated network-fork risks, larger blocks increase storage as well as bandwidth requirements (Bonneau et al., 2015). As a result, more users might switch to operating Simplified Payment Verification (SPV) nodes. SPV nodes only download block headers instead of the entire network copy and rely on full nodes for transaction verification (Gebraselase et al., 2021). This switch, in turn, would centralize the network and weaken its security (Buterin, 2014).

Sharding, a specific Layer-1 approach, splits up the blockchain into smaller partitions for more efficient transaction processing. While sharding speeds up transactions, it also fragments security resources, increases the attack surface, and introduces complexities in cross-shard communication (Liu et al., 2022). Notably, Ethereum has moved away from sharding toward Layer-2 solutions as the community deems them more effective (Ethereum, 2023f).

Layer-2 solutions process transactions off-chain, reducing the load on the main blockchain. As such, the transaction throughput can be significantly increased without altering the base layer (Gangwal et al., 2023). Prominent Layer-2 solutions include sidechains and rollups: Sidechains, on the one hand, are auxiliary blockchains with their own security protocols that operate in parallel to the main network. Yet, this approach requires bridges between the networks, for example to transfer assets, which could become central points of control and vulnerability.

Rollups, on the other hand, execute transactions off-chain and post a summarized version back to the main chain, benefiting from the base layer's security. However, the entities managing rollups could become centralized, potentially influencing the network's integrity (Sguanci et al., 2021).

It can be concluded that, while Layer-1 and Layer-2 solutions offer effective solutions to increase the transaction throughput per second in blockchain networks, they still face challenges in maintaining a balance between scalability, security, and decentralization. The perfect equilibrium within the trilemma has yet to be achieved.

2.2.5 Blockchain Types

The fundamental principle of a decentralized ledger is consistent across different blockchain implementations. However, the architecture, accessibility, and governance of the implementations can vary significantly, as noted by Shrestha et al. (2020). Guegan (2017) categorizes blockchains into two primary types: public and private networks, which each have their own advantages and disadvantages. For a concise comparison of public and private blockchains, refer to Table 2.1. This table sets the stage for a more detailed exploration of these network types in the subsequent sections.

Table 2.1 Types of Blockchain Networks

Class	Type	Read	Update the Ledger	Example
Public	Permissionless	Anyone	Anyone	Bitcoin, Ethereum
	Permissioned	Anyone	Authorized participants	Sovrin
Private	Consortium	Authorized participants	Authorized participants	Multiple banks operating a shared ledger
	Permissioned	Authorized participants	Network operator only	Internal bank ledger shared among parent company and subsidiaries

Source: Adapted from Hileman and Rauchs (2017), p. 20

2.2.5.1 Public Blockchains

Public blockchains are open networks that grant anyone the ability to join the network and view all recorded transactions (Oh & Shong, 2017). Their decentralized nature prevents any single entity from exerting control, thereby promoting resistance to censorship and enhancing security against malicious attacks (Prasad et al., 2018). However, the immutability of these blockchains, while a strength, can also be a challenge: Once transactions are added to the blockchain, they cannot be altered retroactively, even if they are erroneous or fraudulent (Clohessy & Acton, 2019).

Public blockchains are differentiated into two types. The first are public permissionless blockchains, where all participants can engage in the transaction validation process, as seen with Bitcoin and Ethereum. The second are public permissioned blockchains like the Sovrin network. Such blockchains allow public data access but restrict participation in the transaction validation to a set of authorized nodes (Hileman & Rauchs, 2017).

2.2.5.2 Private Blockchains

In private blockchains, administrators control network participation and roles, as noted by Prasad et al. (2018). This control extends to write permissions, allowing them to grant selective access where some users can view all data but cannot add transactions (Guegan, 2017). Perera et al. (2020) highlight that this selective access is key to the high level of privacy in these networks. Private networks are categorized into two types: First, there are private permissioned networks, which are managed by a single organization. Such a network could, for example, be an internal bank ledger shared among a parent company and its subsidiaries.

Second, there are consortium-based networks, in which a group of organizations collaboratively manages the network. An example could be multiple banks operating a shared ledger, as Hileman and Rauchs (2017) illustrate. Noteworthy architectures in this realm include Hyperledger Fabric and R3 Corda, as outlined by Valenta and Sandner (2017).

Given that participant identities are verified, there is no need for complex consensus mechanisms, which allows for faster transaction processing. Coupled with the ability to tailor the blockchain to an organization's specific requirements, private blockchains may, according Dinh et al. (2017), hold considerable promise in revolutionizing the highly regulated banking and financial sector. However, the setup comes at the expense of a reduction in decentralization, potentially leading to vulnerabilities toward a single point of failure (Shrestha et al., 2020). Moreover, by design, transparency is restricted, which limits the ability of external parties to audit or verify transactions (Perera et al., 2020).

2.2.6 Smart Contracts

One central feature of the Ethereum blockchain is its support for smart contracts (Buterin, 2014). Initially conceptualized by computer scientist Nick Szabo in the 1990s, smart contracts automatically enforce and execute contract terms when predetermined conditions are fulfilled (Szabo, 1997). As a result, the need for trusted intermediaries can be eliminated, and the risk for a single point of failure can be minimized, which increases the system's resilience (Buterin, 2014). It is possible to bundle different smart contracts into so-called "decentralized applications," or "dApps," which are programs that run on the blockchain. This feature also makes it possible to execute complex transactions automatically (Wu et al., 2021).

In practice, setting up a smart contract on Ethereum requires that the involved parties agree on the terms, which are then encoded into the blockchain. Subsequent modifications to the contract are governed by predefined rules within the contract's code (Buterin, 2014). When a triggering event occurs, such as the delivery of goods, the contract's code is executed to transfer assets accordingly and record the transaction on the blockchain (Mukherjee & Pradhan, 2021).

The Ethereum Virtual Machine (EVM), which is the core computing engine that powers the Ethereum platform, enables the deployment and execution of smart contracts. It also provides a secure and isolated environment that ensures that contracts run precisely as programmed, which mitigates risks like downtime, censorship, and fraud. This feature contributes to Ethereum's reliability as a platform for a wide range of dApps. Ethereum's programming language is Turing-complete, which means that it can theoretically execute any computable function. However, in practice, factors like transaction costs and network capacity may impose limits on the complexity of operations that can be performed (Buterin, 2014).

2.2.7 Tokenization

In the realm of blockchain technology, tokenization refers to the process of representing data or assets, both physical and virtual, in the form of a unique character sequence, commonly known as a "token" (Morrow & Zarrebini, 2019). A token acts as a reference to an asset and does not contain any economic value or sensitive data itself, as highlighted by Wang and Nixon (2021). Essentially, there are two different types of tokens: fungible and non-fungible tokens, with the latter also abbreviated as *"NFTs"* (Fairfield, 2022). Fungible tokens are interchangeable and indistinguishable units of value, like cryptocurrencies as Bitcoin. Each fungible token holds the same value and characteristics as any other unit of the same token (Kugler, 2021).

In contrast, NFTs are unique digital assets that are verified on a blockchain. Each NFT represents distinct values or properties, which makes them irreplaceable and different from any other token (Schaer, 2021). Both types of tokens act as digital proofs of ownership or entitlement (Levis et al., 2021). To enhance interoperability, token standards have been introduced. For instance, the Ethereum blockchain utilizes the ERC-20 standard, which specifies a uniform set of rules and functions that tokens on its network must implement. This standardization ensures that tokens can interact seamlessly with other tokens and smart contracts, facilitating a more integrated and efficient ecosystem (Ethereum, 2023a).

Tokenization of real-world assets has garnered significant attention in blockchain research because it offers numerous benefits (Juan et al., 2023). One of the main advantages is the elimination of most intermediate financial, legal and regulatory bodies, leading to substantially reduced transaction costs (Wang & Nixon, 2021). As such, the underlying asset can be traded P2P (OECD, 2019). Moreover, it democratizes access to assets, allowing for a broader range of participants in the market: For instance, assets that were traditionally illiquid or inaccessible to the average investor, such as real estate or intellectual property, can be tokenized and fractionally owned by multiple parties (OECD, 2019). This advantage not only opens up new investment opportunities but also enhances the liquidity of historically illiquid markets (OECD, 2020).

However, according to Wang and Nixon (2021) the evolution of tokenization on the blockchain is still in its nascent stage: While the potential is vast, numerous technological and regulatory challenges and risks need to be addressed. Consequently, ensuring compliance for tokenized real assets requires regulatory clarity, which has not yet been extensively provided (Wang & Nixon, 2021). Moreover, a reliable method is needed for aligning on-chain tokens with off-chain assets because unpredictable off-chain events must be adequately reflected on the blockchain (Uzsoki, 2019). Furthermore, a certain level of interoperability between blockchain systems would allow for digital assets to be seamlessly exchanged across different platforms, which would then enhance the utility and value of tokenized assets (OECD, 2020).

In conclusion, tokenization on blockchains presents a revolutionary approach to asset ownership and management. By converting tangible and intangible assets into digital tokens, the blockchain ecosystem offers enhanced transparency and accessibility. The potential to democratize asset ownership, reduce transaction costs, and introduce new investment opportunities is immense. However, realizing the full potential of tokenization requires a concerted effort from different stakeholders, such as technologists or regulators, to address the existing challenges and pave the way for a future underpinned by tokenization.

2.2.8 Blockchain Applications

Since its inception, blockchain technology has emerged as one of the most transformative innovations in the digital realm. Due to its inherent technological attributes, blockchain technology has the potential to disrupt a diverse spectrum of operational processes. As a result, Efanov and Roschin (2018) see it "as the most significant invention after the internet" (p. 116).

This view is supported by Alam et al. (2021), who emphasize that blockchain technology could be applied anywhere an external entity is needed to verify transactions, indicating its vast applicability across various sectors. Yang (2019) attributes much potential to blockchain in streamlining processes and eliminating paperwork, which could revolutionize traditional workflows. Building upon these insights, the observation of AlShamsi et al. (2022) that a substantial portion of contemporary blockchain research focuses on supply chain management applications suggests that this domain holds significant promise. Furthermore, Abou Jaoude and Saade (2019) extend this perspective by outlining how sectors such as the internet of things (IoT), energy, healthcare, government, and finance could greatly profit from blockchain implementation, highlighting the technology's transformative potential across a broad spectrum of industries.

The application of blockchain technology today has progressed through a series of phases, commonly delineated as Blockchain 1.0 to Blockchain 4.0. This tiered classification, first introduced by Swan (2015) and subsequently elaborated on by Mukherjee and Pradhan (2021) as well as Chang et al. (2022), segments the technology's evolution into distinct phases. Each phase introduced novel functionalities and applications.

Efanov and Roschin (2018) describe the first three phases as follows: "Blockchain 1.0 as digital currency, Blockchain 2.0 as digital economy, and Blockchain 3.0 as digital society" (p. 117). However, "Blockchain 1.0 took a few years to mature starting from 2008, Blockchain 2.0 and 3.0 have emerged almost in parallel in an explosive manner around 2015" (Zhao et al., 2016, p. 1). Blockchain 4.0 is the most recent development. With reference to Mukherjee and Pradhan (2021), the quote may possibly be supplemented as follows: "Blockchain 4.0 as digital ecosystem."

The initial phase, Blockchain 1.0, centered on transactional activities, implementing digital currency applications like Bitcoin (Efanov & Roschin, 2018). It introduced the concept of decentralized digital money, eliminating the need for intermediaries like banks and emphasizing P2P transactions using cryptographic principles (Nakamoto, 2008).

The second phase, Blockchain 2.0, expanded the technology's horizons beyond mere transactions to diverse financial and economic implementations (Burgess & Colangelo, 2015). Especially the introduction of smart contracts has spurred diverse applications: As such, blockchain could significantly reduce costs and address trust and transparency issues in supply chain finance programs (Zhang et al., 2021). These programs enable early invoice payments for suppliers while simultaneously extending payment terms for buyers (Hofmann, 2011).

Moreover, by applying smart contracts in financial transactions, trust-based systems like clearinghouses could be replaced, as the transfers are executed in an "all-or-nothing" manner. That approach not only reduces settlement risk, but also increases transaction efficiency (Schaer, 2021). By means of tokenization, these benefits might also be directly transferable to applications such as stock trading (Bhandarkar et al., 2019).

The third phase, Blockchain 3.0, commenced almost simultaneously with the second (Zhao et al., 2016). It introduced a wide range of applications extending beyond finance and commerce (Burgess & Colangelo, 2015). For example, it can be used in supply chains to ensure transparency and traceability, providing an immutable record of product movements (Gurtu & Johny, 2019); in energy grids, to facilitate P2P trading, enabling real-time settlements and eliminating intermediary transaction costs (Esmat et al., 2021); in healthcare, to track patient medical history, ensuring completeness, privacy and security in electronic health records (Tanwar et al., 2020); in governmental processes, to provide secure and tamper-proof infrastructure for identity management (Sullivan & Burger, 2017) or voting (Moura & Gomes, 2017); as well as in complementing IoT solutions, to improve interoperability between systems, reliability and data privacy (Dai et al., 2019).

Blockchain 4.0 represents the latest advancement in blockchain technology, as described by Angelis and Da Silva (2019). This stage involves the creation of business ecosystems through cross-communication between different protocols and the integration of multiple technologies (Mukherjee & Pradhan, 2021). Angelis and Da Silva (2019) emphasize the integration of blockchain technology with AI, such as using blockchain to securely store outcomes from AI applications. Yet, according to Mukherjee and Pradhan (2021), such solutions are still in their infancy. Seeking competitive advantages such as cost savings and increased efficiency, many companies are currently investing and innovating in blockchain technology. As a result, this development can be expected to continue (Levis et al., 2021).

2.2.9 Challenges in Blockchain Implementation

As just outlined, blockchain technology's decentralized structure, immutability, and transparency make it a compelling solution for a wide range of applications beyond cryptocurrencies. However, like any emerging technology, blockchain faces several challenges and implementation barriers that must be addressed to unlock its full potential (Weerawarna et al., 2023).

In line with Batubara et al. (2018), this paper will use the "Technology—Organization—Environment" framework to systematically categorize identified challenges. This framework, initially developed by Tornatzky et al. (1990), offers a structured method for understanding the complexities of adopting new technologies within organizations and the broader market environment.

2.2.9.1 Technological Challenges

One of the most pressing challenges for blockchain technology is to scale efficiently. So far, not being able to enable high transaction rates per second without significantly compromising on the system's security and decentralization (as detailed in 2.2.4) has impeded widespread blockchain implementation (Sharma et al., 2022).

In their discussion of blockchain-based healthcare applications, Agbo et al. (2019) identify the lack of standardization and interoperability among different blockchain systems as a significant implementation barrier. This absence of uniformity and compatibility leads to inefficiencies, particularly in scenarios that require cross-chain communication or transactions.

Porru et al. (2017) emphasize that traditional software development practices are inadequate for blockchain. This inadequacy, which presents a significant challenge, is due to the need for new tools and techniques that are still developing. A notable example underscoring this gap in development maturity was "the DAO" incident in June 2016. In this case, a vulnerability in a smart contract on the Ethereum blockchain was exploited, resulting in a loss of approximately US$50 million to US$60 million in ETH. This led to a controversial "hard fork" of the network, splitting the blockchain to create a new version to recover the funds. Furthermore, Esmaeilian et al. (2020) and Weerawarna et al. (2023) identify the significant energy consumption associated with blockchain as a barrier to its widespread implementation.

2.2.9.2 Organizational Challenges

Organizational barriers encompass challenges within both inter-organizational and intra-organizational contexts (Saberi et al., 2019). In the inter-organizational domain, one critical issue is the establishment of trust and the preservation of anonymity, as highlighted by Weerawarna et al. (2023). Consequently, linking a user's identity to a public blockchain application could raise significant data privacy concerns, especially if such information becomes accessible to all application users (von Haller Gronbaek, 2016).

With regard to intra-organizational barriers, organizations may be hesitant to adopt new technologies because their reliability is yet to be proven (Batubara et al., 2018). The implementation of blockchain technology also requires considerable resources, particularly financial, as noted by Mishra et al. (2023). Furthermore, challenges such as a lack of sufficient training or knowledge among employees and inadequate management support can impede the effective implementation of blockchain technology (Walsh et al., 2021).

2.2.9.3 Environmental Challenges

Blockchain literature highlights several "environmental" or external challenges to blockchain adoption. This category includes the erosion of public trust, a concern amplified by incidents such as the "the DAO" attack previously mentioned (Yeoh, 2017). Sharma et al. (2022) build upon this observation by underscoring the imperative for company- and government-led regulations to mend this trust. They draw attention to a particularly pronounced obstacle in the effective implementation of blockchain: regulatory uncertainty. As summarized by Batubara et al. (2018), when talking about blockchain adoption, "laws and regulatory support are essential and should ensure that a user has legal certainty as to the law to determine the rights and obligations of the parties to the agreement and which courts will handle any disputes" (p. 6).

The enforceability of smart contracts is uncertain across various jurisdictions, which raises questions about the legal status of crypto assets and their recognition as property (OECD, 2020). Notably, the United Kingdom (UK) has proposed a new property law category for crypto assets (Law Commission, 2023), and Hong Kong has recognized them as property capable of being held in trust (Hogan Lovells, 2023), signaling a shift toward legal clarity.

The integration of blockchain into existing legal frameworks presents challenges, such as aligning legal rights with blockchain records and reconciling centralized legal processes with decentralized technologies (Schuster, 2021). Regulatory approaches vary significantly, with the European Union (EU) rather favoring innovation-friendly policies, while the United States of America (U.S.) have adopted a more cautious stance to address emerging risks (Yeoh, 2017).

Burgess and Colangelo (2015) urge prudence in introducing regulations so that they are not overly burdensome or too detrimental to blockchain's privacy features. As such, they call on regulators to adopt a nuanced approach—treating different blockchain applications based on their individual characteristics rather than employing a blanket regulatory framework—to avoid undesirable consequences. Additionally, Levis et al. (2021) emphasize the importance of industrial players and regulators comprehending and navigating the potential of blockchain technology for optimal economic outcomes. They caution that missteps in this regard could even diminish a country's industrial competitiveness and productivity.

2.3 Blockchain-Based Bonds

The integration of blockchain technology into financial instruments like corporate bonds could significantly transform their issuance, management, and trading. Blockchain-based bonds, leveraging the technology's inherent characteristics, are primarily expected to enhance transparency and efficiency. This advancement could not only revolutionize investor relations management and trading mechanisms but also impact the overall structure of the financial sector.

This chapter delves into merging traditional bonds with blockchain, examining how this integration could theoretically streamline bond-market operations. It also provides an in-depth overview of the current regulatory landscape, with a specific focus on Germany's pioneering efforts through the Electronic Securities Act of 2021. Finally, the chapter synthesizes academic literature on the use of blockchain in securities, offering insights into empirical evidence, practical applications, and the evolving narrative of blockchain-based bond adoption.

2.3.1 Theoretical Framework

Drawing from the in-depth study of corporate bonds and blockchain technology, this section methodically evaluates the implications across the bond lifecycle when merging the two concepts. It details a theoretical framework within a blockchain-based environment, concentrating on general principles and deliberately not delving into country-specific legal nuances at this stage.

The impact of blockchain on the corporate-bond lifecycle initiates at the issuance stage, where its integration promises to transform traditional practices. Recording details such as issuer information, terms, conditions, and payment schedules on an immutable ledger might enhance both trust and transparency.

The P2P nature of blockchain technology could cause a shift away from the traditional role of investment banks in bond issuance, potentially reducing their intermediary functions. This change might lead to increased efficiency in the issuance process. Nevertheless, adhering to regulatory standards, such as know your customer (KYC) and anti-money laundering (AML) regulations, remains an essential requirement. In a system without intermediaries, the responsibility to ensure compliance would likely shift to the issuers and investors themselves.

As the bond progresses through its lifecycle, the advantages of blockchain technology become increasingly evident. Particularly in the settlement phase, the adoption of real-time settlement mechanisms, such as instant delivery versus payment (DvP) systems, facilitates more efficient transaction execution while reducing both risks and costs. When assets and cash are both digitized on the chain, concurrent execution of securities and payment transactions is enabled. This advancement affects primary and secondary financial markets alike. As a result, traditional clearinghouses, which currently play a critical role in transaction facilitation and risk mitigation, might experience a significant shift in their operational roles.

Post-issuance, the blockchain's ability to maintain a detailed and current transaction history becomes crucial. Its immutability guarantees the permanence of recorded transactions. This characteristic could reduce reliance on CSDs because it enables the secure storage and documentation of bonds on the blockchain, thus eliminating the need for physical storage solutions.

Moreover, by disclosing the public keys of the wallets involved in a transaction, transparency can be achieved while simultaneously preserving anonymity. This possibility suggests that bond transactions can be perpetually monitored and verified on the blockchain without revealing the stakeholders' identities. Consequently, adoption might introduce a superior level of security and confidentiality to bond transactions, yet in keeping with the limits of KYC and AML requirements.

Approaching maturity, integrating smart contracts within bond management underscores the transformative potential of blockchain technology. By encoding the terms of bonds, such as interest rates and maturity dates, into smart contracts, these digital agreements could autonomously execute repayments and enforce other contractual conditions once predetermined criteria are met. This automation, if set up properly, has the potential to minimize the need for manual oversight and reduce the likelihood of human error.

In summary, the integration of blockchain technology fundamentally transforms the corporate-bond lifecycle from issuance to maturity. It introduces unprecedented levels of efficiency, security, and transparency. Additionally, by potentially redefining or even eliminating the role of some intermediaries in the bond issuance and management process, it could streamline operations and reduce costs.

2.3.2 Regulatory Framework

This section analyzes Germany's regulatory approach to blockchain in corporate bond issuances, underscoring the importance of its Electronic Securities Act. The study notes developments in EU member states, like Luxembourg, with its Blockchain Acts (LFF, 2023), and non-EU countries, such as Switzerland, with its DLT bill (SFC, 2021). Nevertheless, the focus on Germany reflects the country's significant role as a major EU economy. Germany's regulatory approach within the EU context provides valuable insights into the integration of blockchain in financial markets, making it a key case study for understanding the interplay between national and EU-wide regulations.

Germany's Electronic Securities Act, abbreviated as *"eWpG" ("Gesetz ueber elektronische Wertpapiere")*, was enacted in June 2021. It has significantly advanced the regulatory landscape for blockchain-based bonds in Germany. The eWpG abolishes the requirement for physical certificates in securities trading, thereby simplifying the tokenization of securities. Although security tokenization had already been feasible before the introduction of the eWpG, the legal mandate for a corresponding physical document created obstacles (Cashlink, 2021). This new legislation permits blockchain-based bonds to be considered equivalent to traditional bonds, provided they adhere to defined criteria. Equal consideration means that they fall under the Markets in Financial Instruments Directive II (MiFID II) and the Markets in Financial Instruments Regulation (MiFIR), which set the EU-wide framework for investment services and market transparency (EU, 2014a, 2014c).

To qualify as equivalent to traditional bonds, such bonds, along with their details, must be registered with either a traditional CSD *("Zentralregister")* or a decentralized crypto securities register *("Kryptowertpapierregister")*. While the crypto register is technology-neutral, its requirements for tamper-proof record-keeping and sequential data logging align well with blockchain technology capabilities. The operation of this crypto register necessitates a designated registrar that is responsible for ensuring that the electronic register accurately reflects the current legal status, including the ownership structure. It must also guarantee precise entries and transfers and provide robust protection against data loss or unauthorized modifications, as outlined in the Electronic Securities Act (eWpG, 2021).

However, it is important to note that under the EU's Central Securities Depositories Regulation (CSDR), a bond is only eligible for exchange trading if it is held in central custody (EU, 2014b). This regulation presents a notable consideration for blockchain-based bonds, as it defines the conditions under which these bonds can be traded on regulated markets.

In October 2022, Germany introduced the *eWpRV ("Verordnung ueber Anforderungen an elektronische Wertpapierregister"),* an ordinance refining the eWpG. It details the standards for maintaining electronic securities registries, particularly regarding authentication tools and cryptographic methods used, as well as the essential information to be included in the register (eWpRV, 2022).

Another pivotal German regulation is the German Banking Act, abbreviated as *"KWG" ("Kreditwesengesetz").* Any entity engaging in the issuance, management, or trading of bonds—either traditional or blockchain-based—must ensure compliance with these regulations, which emphasizes the KWG's role in shaping blockchain's trajectory in the German financial sector.

Beyond the established guidelines for KYC and AML procedures, risk management, consumer protection, and data integrity, the KWG introduces additional regulatory requirements. Among these are licensing mandates for entities involved in crypto securities-registry management *("Kryptowertpapierregisterfuehrung")* and crypto custody services, which include maintaining wallets for storing assets on behalf of owners *("Kryptoverwahrgeschaeft").* Companies aspiring to offer these services must obtain a license from the German Federal Financial Supervisory Authority, BaFin (KWG, 1998).

In the context of these national regulations, it is also essential to consider the role of the Basel Committee on Banking Supervision (BCBS). The BCBS is a central banking regulatory authority that issues guidelines and standards on the supervision of banks. While the Committee has no formal supranational supervisory authority, BCBS member countries are expected to implement its guidelines and standards in their domestic regulations (BCBS, 2018). Hence, it is crucial to closely monitor the organization's decisions.

Effective beginning in 2025, the BCBS has introduced a new standard for the prudential treatment of crypto asset exposures, including blockchain-based bonds, by categorizing them into two groups. Assets that meet established legal, regulatory, as well as operational criteria—such as those regarding network stability and design—and have a risk profile similar to traditional instruments, will be classified under Group 1. These assets will be subject to the same capital requirements as traditional assets under the Basel Framework. Capital requirements, established for banks and financial institutions to mitigate the risk of insolvency, specify the minimum amount of equity that must be maintained as a safeguard against the risks associated with their assets. Conversely, instruments that do not meet these criteria will fall under Group 2, facing stricter capital requirements due to their higher perceived risk (BCBS, 2022).

In December 2023, the BCBS reaffirmed its stance that assets issued on public blockchains are exposed to specific risks that, as of now, cannot be effectively mitigated. These risks include, but are not limited to, concerns related to settlement finality. As a result, such assets are currently not eligible for inclusion in Group 1 (BCBS, 2023). However, the future development of the BCBS recommendations and their implementation at the national level remains to be seen.

Another significant regulatory development at the European level, particularly relevant to blockchain-based bonds, is the DLT Pilot Regime. This initiative is a key component of the European Commission's Digital Finance Package and aims to integrate DLT within the EU's financial markets. Launched in 2023, the Regime is designed to facilitate the testing and observation of DLT in market infrastructures (EU, 2022). It operates within a regulatory "sandbox" (ESMA, 2022, p. 12) that provides a structured environment for experimenting with DLT-based business models. Notably, this sandbox includes trading of decentralized instruments that are not held in central custody, offering a temporary exemption from certain aspects of the CSDR (Freshfields, 2023).

Initially set for a three-year duration, the DLT Pilot Regime can be extended up to six years. Its primary goal is to foster technological innovation, especially in trading and settlement, while maintaining the integrity and regulatory standards of the EU's financial systems. To this end, the Regime introduces new market infrastructures for DLT-based securities, including multilateral trading facilities (MTFs) for trading, settlement systems (SS) for transaction processing, as well as trading and settlement systems (TSS) that combine both services. This framework enables secondary-market trading for DLT-based securities. Operators of these infrastructures are required to work closely with the competent authorities and the European Securities and Markets Authority (ESMA), provide transparent information to clients, and maintain robust IT and cybersecurity measures to ensure service security and reliability (EU, 2022).

The DLT Pilot Regime is specific about its scope. It limits the total volume of DLT-based securities in the sandbox to €6 billion and sets criteria for the eligibility of financial instruments. For instance, the issuance size of bonds must be under €1 billion to mitigate potential systemic risks (EU, 2022).

Overall, the DLT Pilot Regime might be described as an adaptive regulatory approach by the EU that balances the promotion of innovation in digital finance with prudent risk management and sets a potential benchmark for the integration of DLT into financial-market regulation.

Additionally, the Markets in Crypto Assets Regulation (MiCA) is poised to significantly influence the European regulatory framework for crypto assets. To be implemented in 2024, MiCA is another element of the European Commission's Digital Finance Package (ESMA, 2022). It introduces detailed guidelines for crypto-asset service providers, emphasizing stringent custody and safekeeping protocols to protect investors. Notably, MiCA exempts crypto assets that fall under existing regulatory frameworks (EU, 2023). As a result, any blockchain-based bond that falls under MiFID II will not be subject to MiCA.

In summary, Germany's regulatory landscape for blockchain-based bonds is advanced and integrative, particularly with the eWpG and eWpRV. They facilitate the issuance and registration of electronic securities, allowing them to be treated on par with traditional securities when certain conditions are met. As recommendations of the BCBS might be translated into national regulation, developments must be closely monitored. At the European level, the DLT Pilot Regime provides a sandbox for DLT in financial markets, aiming to balance innovation with risk management. The MiCA regulation is expected to further harmonize the approach to digital finance across the EU; however, it will not affect blockchain-based bonds that fall under MiFID II.

2.3.3 Related Work

Blockchain and DLT have garnered significant attention within the ecosystem of securities and capital markets. It is crucial to reiterate that academic literature often uses the terms "blockchain" and "DLT" interchangeably. Recognizing this, the search for pertinent studies and publications for the present study expanded to include the wider scope of DLT, not just blockchain. Considering the relatively nascent stage of the discipline, the research scope was broadened to encompass securities at large, rather than exclusively focusing on bonds. As bonds are a subset of securities, they inherently share key characteristics and market dynamics prevalent in the overall securities market, such as risk factors and regulatory frameworks. This commonality suggests that findings broadly relevant to securities are likely to be applicable to bonds as well. Therefore, this section provides a succinct overview of key studies that explore DLT's and blockchain's impact on the issuance and lifecycle of securities, along with related regulatory considerations.

Petrov (2019) conducted a thorough analysis of blockchain and DLT applications in financial services, including capital markets. His study highlights key challenges and opportunities, culminating in recommendations to maximize the technology's potential in the sector. Earlier, Pinna and Ruttenberg (2016) dedicated their research to evaluating how the core characteristics of DLTs might drive their adoption within financial institutions and examined their potential impact on the post-trade landscape for European securities. This work has laid the groundwork for many subsequent studies in this domain.

Building on that work, Mortensen (2021) assessed the adoption patterns of DLT in financial markets. His exploration details DLT's burgeoning influence on post-trade processes and points to the rise of digital assets and central bank digital currencies (CBDCs), potentially serving as a catalyst for wider blockchain implementation.

Collomb and Sok (2016) analyzed the transformative impact of blockchain and DLT on capital markets and corporations within the financial sector while expressing concerns about blockchain's scalability and interoperability issues. They anticipate a cautious integration of DLT in capital markets due to existing complexities. This assessment aligns with both (a) Casey et al. (2018), who acknowledge blockchain's potential while emphasizing scalability and privacy challenges as well as the need for cross-organization coordination and (b) Santo et al. (2016), who pinpoint immediate technical hurdles but also see the transformative promise of applying DLT to capital markets. That is why Santo et al. (2016) advocates for a hands-on approach to realize industry-wide efficiencies and cost savings.

Delving into the challenges, Mori (2016) asserts that only 20% of the barriers are technology-based, while a significant 80% are rooted in existing business processes and models. Nevertheless, he estimates that full blockchain integration in financial systems is likely to be achieved within a decade. Popescu (2020) highlights that the tokenization of assets like corporate bonds can reshape capital markets by increasing liquidity and making pricing more transparent. At the same time, he calls for prompt updates to regulatory and tax guidelines to account for matters that are not covered in current frameworks. Despite optimism, Lee (2018) warns that benefits like reduced costs might not materialize as expected and emphasized a continued need for central authorities despite DLT's decentralized nature.

Bauvars and Kirikova (2021) propose a three-layer model for blockchain-based securities settlement, emphasizing that real-world implementation would be intricate, demanding long implementation time and broad market commitment at the same time. A Capgemini whitepaper, authored by Vakta et al. (2016), illuminates the inefficiencies of traditional securities issuances, like bonds. They advocate for using blockchain to digitally represent securities and leverage smart contracts for process automation. This approach should reduce cost in bond issuance and provide faster settlements as well as auditable records. Their conclusion is consistent with Pana and Gangal (2021), who emphasized blockchain technology's potential to optimize bonds throughout their lifecycle, particularly in cost, reporting, and settlement. Yet, they underscore the lack of regulatory clarity and standardization, as well as trust issues.

Another whitepaper by Cashlink (2021) contrasts crypto securities that are in line with the eWpG with security tokens and traditional securities. It spotlights the fact that, in terms of efficiency, crypto securities outperform security tokens—especially with respect to regulatory security and attraction of new investors—as well as traditional securities. In contrast, Saramago (2022) highlights that DLT-based issuances are not inherently cheaper, quicker, or less complex. Using data from two transactions, she conducted a comparative study of DLT-based and traditional bond issuances. Yet, she notes that the case study methodology might limit the scope of her conclusions.

In their quantitative research, Bauer et al. (2023) assessed the cost-saving potential of DLT within capital market infrastructures. Their findings indicated that, by 2028, DLT could reduce expenses in middle- and back-office operations by over 85% compared to existing systems. The study also reveals that, already within the current operational setup, DLT might lead to a decrease in operational costs by approximately 22%.

In addition, the application of blockchain in the context of green bonds, in particular, is attracting attention in academic research: Malamas et al. (2020) propose a blockchain architecture for green bond issuances, ensuring enhanced traceability and auditability of eco-friendly project funds. Their digitized process specifically addresses the unique transparency needs of green bonds. Christodoulou et al. (2023) add a unique perspective by discussing "greenwashing" in the European Union green bonds (EUGB) market, proposing a blockchain-based solution to ensure the authenticity of green projects while reducing monitoring cost at the same time. Axelsen et al. (2023) address the challenges of certification and scalable infrastructure in voluntary carbon credit markets by proposing a DLT TSS for green bonds under the EU DLT Pilot Regime. Their research suggests that DLT can enhance transparency, security, and efficiency, challenging conventional capital markets.

Regulation and governance stand at the forefront of the discourse. Casey et al. (2018) emphasize not only the technical challenges accompanying blockchain implementation, but also the imperative of aligning blockchain endeavors with existing public policy frameworks, referencing insights from ongoing U.S. regulatory debates. Lehmann (2021) highlights the inconsistent private-law frameworks for blockchain across countries and advocates for global harmonization, led by entities like UNIDROIT or the EU, to protect blockchain's utility and investor interests.

This view is in line with a UBS whitepaper authored by Choudhury et al. (2023), which points to the experimental stage of DLT-based securities in capital markets, warning that inconsistent regulatory landscapes could hinder the development of a widespread DLT ecosystem. Ratna et al. (2019) outlined the fragmented U.S. regulation of virtual assets, driving blockchain startups to countries like Singapore and Switzerland. They stress that the U.S.'s lack of a unified approach could limit its potential in the blockchain domain.

Priem (2020) examined DLT's potential in European securities clearing and settlement, noting efficiency benefits alongside significant regulatory challenges, especially compliance with the European Market Infrastructure Regulation (EMIR). He stressed the need for balanced regulation to ensure fairness among financial service providers. Zaccaroni (2022) studied the DLT Pilot Regime's effects on financial market roles. He concluded that, while it encourages some decentralization, the EU continues to lean toward protective standards that can be perceived as innovation barriers. While established firms may be primed for DLT adoption, newer blockchain-centric companies might grapple with regulatory challenges, suggesting a potential advantage in collaborative ventures between the two types of companies.

While DLT's potential for transforming capital markets and securities is a topical subject, much of the existing discourse remains on a theoretical level. This emphasis on theory poses challenges in evaluating the actual implementation of blockchain in capital markets, particularly in bond markets. It hinders a clear understanding of the driving factors, the issues faced in real transactions, and the practical perspectives on the future of blockchain-based bonds. To bridge this gap, this research employs expert interviews, aiming to offer a thorough and nuanced understanding of the current landscape and development trajectory of blockchain-based bonds.

Methodology 3

3.1 Expert Interview Approach

In this study, 19 experts from banking, fintech, industrial corporations, and asset management were interviewed to explore the impact of blockchain-based bonds on corporate financing and their potential to reshape the bond market. The focus was on assessing comparative aspects of blockchain-based and traditional bonds, perceived benefits and barriers, the transformational role of blockchain in market intermediaries and infrastructure, and expert projections on the future trajectory of blockchain-based bonds.

Experts, primarily holding senior positions and based in Germany, were selected for the study. The interviews were conducted virtually and accommodated the participants' schedules and language preferences, utilizing a semi-structured approach. This approach was based on a comprehensive questionnaire, which was crafted following a literature review and preliminary discussions with the project team and banks involved in Siemens's blockchain-based bond issuance.

For the analysis of the interview data, a combination of Mayring's deductive and inductive category building, along with summative content analysis, was employed. This method facilitated a systematic and comprehensive interpretation of the qualitative data. It enabled in-depth exploration of the ways in which blockchain-based bonds are reshaping corporate financing and altering market dynamics. Employing this combined analytical approach provided a nuanced understanding of the complex and evolving landscape surrounding blockchain-based bonds.

M. M. Grossmann, *Blockchain-Based Bonds*, BestMasters,
https://doi.org/10.1007/978-3-658-45311-4_3

3.2 Sample Selection

The initial phase of the research involved selecting a diverse and comprehensive group of experts from across a corporate bond's lifecycle.

According to Bogner et al. (2009), experts are persons who have "technical, process and interpretative knowledge that refers to a specific field of action, by virtue of the fact that the expert acts in a relevant way (for example, in a particular organizational field or the experts' own professional area)" (p. 54). This definition is in line with Meuser and Nagel (1991), who describe an expert as someone with a key role in problem-solving or privileged information access, often within an organizational context, whose specific knowledge and experience are particularly relevant.

In this context, especially experts from the following groups were considered relevant: bond issuers, such as treasuries of industrial corporations and banks; transaction facilitators, encompassing both banks and fintechs, to address customer-oriented and technical aspects alike; and the capital market's buy-side, represented by asset managers.

Purposive sampling was employed in this study to select individuals with specific expertise for the interviews, aligning with the study's objectives. This method facilitated an in-depth exploration of complex topics, focusing on the depth and relevance of information rather than on statistical representativeness. As von Soest (2023) notes, "expert judgements are inherently personal and not necessarily representative or replicable" (p. 3). By choosing experts who can offer informed perspectives, purposive sampling ensures the collection of data that is not only rich but also directly relevant to the core aims of qualitative research, as emphasized by Tansey (2007). Consequently, experts from Germany were specifically targeted to match the study's geographical focus, with particular emphasis on those in senior positions. Experts on this level were deemed to possess a profound understanding and strategic insight, which is essential for a thorough analysis of the complexities and potential impacts of blockchain-based bonds.

Initially, this study intended to conduct twelve interviews, following the guidelines for largely homogeneous expert groups as established by Guest et al. (2006). However, the specific complexities and evolving nature of blockchain-based bonds necessitated a modification of this approach. To achieve data saturation and gain a deeper understanding, the number of interviews was pragmatically increased. In line with the approach of Guthoff et al. (2023), saturation was deemed achieved when no new themes had emerged, which occurred after conducting 15 interviews.

Different strategies were employed to acquire interview partners. Leveraging Siemens's extensive network—which includes representatives of banks, fintech companies, other industrial corporations, and asset managers alike—was key in identifying appropriate candidates. Additionally, efforts were made to reach high-ranking executives, especially CEOs, from relevant fintech firms, using either personal or general company email addresses obtained from their websites.

Candidates were sent an official interview invitation via email, which is provided in Fig. 9 in the electronic supplementary material. The email outlined the research objectives and suggested potential interview dates. To ensure comprehensive participation and data collection, follow-up reminders were sent to non-responsive candidates. This systematic approach was crucial in securing a diverse and insightful range of perspectives for the study. Experts who agreed to participate were then provided with the interview questionnaire. However, three potential interviews did not materialize: One candidate was restricted by the compliance department of its corporation, another withdrew citing a lack of sufficient expertise after reviewing the questionnaire, and the third did not respond to the initial invitation or subsequent follow-ups.

Significantly, three interviewees recommended including colleagues from different departments in their respective interviews, leveraging their joint experience in previous blockchain-based bond transactions. Their recommendation, highlighting the interdisciplinary nature of the topic, was adopted to enrich the study's understanding of the process.

Incorporating experts from diverse fields enabled the research to achieve a multifaceted perspective, thoroughly addressing the legal, technical, and operational aspects of blockchain-based bond transactions. This approach ensured a comprehensive examination of all pertinent aspects. The study ultimately compiled insights from 19 experts across 15 interviews. To protect the confidentiality of the interviewees, just the assigned group, the type of their employer company, jurisdiction of employment, and current role are disclosed. Details on the final sample are presented in Table 3.1.

Table 3.1 Final Expert Sample

Expert	Group	Type of Employer Company	Location	Role
1	TF	Private sector bank	UK	Director
2	TF	Fintech	France	Deputy CEO
3	TF	Public sector bank	Germany	Senior Vice President
4	TF	Private sector bank	Germany	Associate Director
5	TF	Private sector bank	Germany	Director
6	BS	Asset manager	Germany	Manager
7	TF	Public sector bank	Germany	Senior Manager
8	TF	Public sector bank	Germany	Consultant
9	TF	Fintech	Luxembourg	CEO
10	TF	Fintech	Germany	Project Manager
11	IS	Private sector bank	UK	Head of Department
12	TF	Private sector bank	Switzerland	Managing Director
13	TF	Fintech	Germany	CEO
14	TF	Private sector bank	Germany	Associate General Counsel
15	TF	Private sector bank	Germany	Managing Director
16	IS	Industrial corporation	Germany	Manager
17	IS	Industrial corporation	Germany	Senior Vice President
18	IS	Industrial corporation	Germany	Senior Manager
19	IS	Industrial corporation	Germany	Senior Legal Counsel

Note: "IS = Bond issuer", TF = "Transaction facilitator", BS = "Capital market's buy-side representative"
Source: Own illustration

3.3 Questionnaire

The expert interviews followed the completion of a comprehensive questionnaire consisting of 15 questions. These questions were primarily developed based on existing literature and insights from preliminary discussions with the project team and banks involved in Siemens's early 2023 blockchain-based bond issuance. This approach ensured the questions were rooted in practical experience while aligning with relevant theoretical frameworks. To verify the suitability and completeness of the interview questions, they underwent a critical review with four experts from the sample prior to the interviews.

To accommodate the characteristics of each expert group, three tailored versions of the questionnaire were created, each with minor modifications (for details, refer to Table 5 in the electronic supplementary material). The questionnaire featured open-ended questions to elicit diverse responses without constraining them to "right" or "wrong" answers. The questions were categorized into three sections, each focusing on a different facet, to ensure comprehensive coverage and facilitate focused responses.

Section A aims to collect fundamental information about the interviewees and their institutions. Respondents are prompted to introduce themselves, outline their current role, and provide details on their institution's involvement in blockchain-based bond issuance or trading. Furthermore, it seeks information on any additional applications of blockchain technology currently being utilized by their institution.

Section B examines blockchain-based bonds, contrasting them with traditional bonds in aspects such as risk, return, client demand, and operational efficiency. It assesses the advantages of blockchain technology in bond issuance and trading as well as factors influencing institutional adoption. This section also identifies appropriate blockchain networks for bond applications and explores their impact on transparency and information flow. Additionally, it addresses technical and regulatory challenges, delving into their effects on scalability and future developments in this sector.

Section C explores the prospective role of blockchain technology in the bond market. It analyzes how blockchain could alter market dynamics, especially in terms of intermediary and infrastructure-provider roles. The section also assesses the long-term viability of blockchain-based bonds as alternatives to traditional bonds and considers the potential for other asset classes to integrate blockchain technology.

3.4 Interview Process

Conducted fully virtually via Microsoft Teams in October and November 2023, the interviews varied in length from 30 to 100 minutes. Although initially anticipated to last 60 minutes, certain interviews necessitated more time. In these cases, the duration was extended, or a follow-up session was scheduled, subject to the interviewees' consent.

This approach ensured a comprehensive exploration of all research topics and questions, thereby enhancing the quality and depth of the data collected.

Interviews were conducted in either English or German, depending on the interviewee's preference.

The interviews adopted a semi-structured approach, in which the questionnaire was flexibly adapted in both wording and sequence, aligning with the evolving flow of each conversation. This method enabled smooth transitions to related topics as they naturally came up, fostering an environment conducive to open communication, and paving the way for the emergence of unexpected insights. The open-ended nature of the questions facilitated comprehensive data collection that was closely aligned with the research objectives. The questionnaire primarily served as a checklist to ensure thorough coverage of all relevant topics while respecting the dynamic nature of the dialogues.

The ethical guidelines outlined in the European Code of Conduct for Research Integrity were strictly adhered to when conducting the interviews. Each interview began with a detailed explanation of the project, emphasizing that responses would be used exclusively for academic research and that the interviewee's anonymity would be ensured. Consent for both recording and transcribing the interviews was explicitly obtained from the participants.

The subsequent transcription of the interviews was conducted using the content-semantic transcription method as outlined by Dresing and Pehl (2015). This approach focuses on capturing the content and meaning of the spoken word. As such, filler words and non-verbal elements are omitted unless they contribute to the overall meaning. The selected method facilitates a deeper analysis of the interview content. Transcriptions were subsequently reviewed by the interviewees for validation, ensuring accurate and authentic representation of their responses. To preserve the integrity of linguistic nuances, the responses were maintained in their original language for the analysis.

3.5 Analysis of the Interviews

The interviews were analyzed using a combination of Mayring's qualitative techniques, tailored to explore the emerging field of blockchain-based bonds. This hybrid approach, outlined in Fig. 3.1, involved a combination of deductive and inductive category building, followed by a summative content analysis (Mayring, 2015). The methodology was selected for its twofold strengths: It provides a clear, structured framework for addressing the research questions, while offering the adaptability necessary to fully capture and accurately represent emerging insights from the expert interviews. The analysis was facilitated using MAXQDA software to enhance the efficiency and organization of the process.

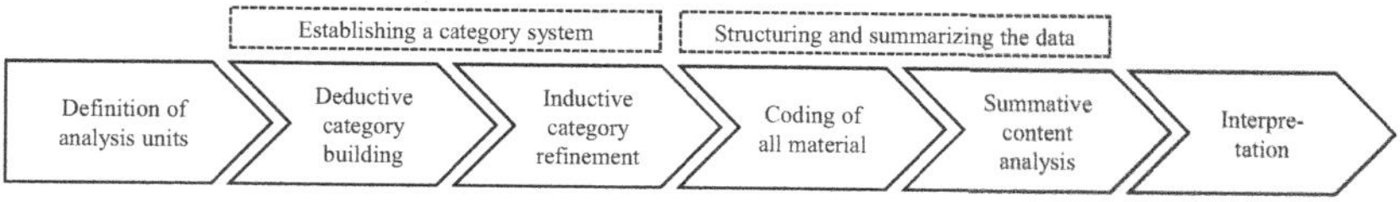

Fig. 3.1 Methodological Approach of the Study. (Source: Own illustration)

The initial phase included preliminary reading of the interview transcripts to establish a foundational understanding of the experts' perspectives in relation to the research questions. Analysis units were defined according to Mayring's guidelines: The Coding Unit, identifying the smallest fragment of text eligible for analysis; the Context Unit, the largest text segment falling under a single category; and the Evaluation Unit, detailing the sequence for examining text portions.

While individual sentences served as the Coding Units, thematically related segments were identified as Context Units to ensure accurate reflection of statements within their proper context. The Evaluation Unit included all 15 interviews as a collective entity. This approach facilitated a comprehensive analysis of the dataset, allowing for an in-depth comparison and synthesis of expert opinions. By considering all interviews as one Evaluation Unit, the analysis focused on identifying overarching themes, patterns, and insights across various expert perspectives.

In the first phase, deductive categories were established based on the research questions and the interview questionnaire. Subsequently, these categories were further refined inductively by analyzing the entire interview transcripts. This method guaranteed that the categories were not only pertinent to the research questions but also adaptable to the collected data set. The iterative process of category refinement involved continuous comparison with the original material to ensure accuracy. Once the category system was established—detailed in Table 6 in the electronic supplementary material—it was systematically applied to code the entire dataset comprehensively.

In the second phase, summative content analysis was applied to synthesize expert opinions from categorized data. This process involved summarizing the categories either directly or through an intermediate reduction step. Considering the substantial volume of data, reduction to the desired level of abstraction was achieved in a single step, in accordance with Mayring's guidelines. The aim was to distill essential content and eliminate superfluous elements. The processed contents were then combined, omitted, or selected based on their relevance and contribution to the research questions.

The findings were structured by category, highlighting key themes and patterns emerging from the interviews. Each category was elaborated with detailed descriptions, enriched by illustrative quotes, which added depth and context. The results were organized to directly address the research questions, thereby crafting a clear and coherent narrative focused on blockchain-based bonds and their associated market structures.

3.6 Quality Criteria

Bogner et al. (2014) highlighted the distinct challenges encountered when attempting to apply traditional quality criteria—objectivity, reliability, and validity, which are staples of quantitative methods—to qualitative research. This distinction arises because qualitative research typically focuses on subjective interpretations, in contrast to the objective, measurable data, which is central to quantitative research. Consequently, these traditional criteria are often considered less appropriate for qualitative studies, prompting a shift toward prioritizing transparency in both the data collection and evaluation processes. In qualitative research, transparency involves a thorough disclosure of the research process and the decision-making journey, acknowledging the inherently interpretative nature of this research approach (Bogner et al., 2014).

In response to this challenge, Mayring (2016) introduced six specific criteria aimed at ensuring the rigor and credibility of qualitative studies. These criteria are specifically designed to accommodate the nuances and complexities inherent in qualitative research. This section explores each of these criteria in detail and how they were applied in this study to ensure the overall quality and integrity of the research:

(1) **Procedural documentation** *("Verfahrensdokumentation"):* The research process was meticulously documented at each stage, including the development of the interview questionnaire, the selection of interview participants, the interview transcription, and the detailed analysis procedures. Notably, for each code in the analysis, code memos were created, comprising descriptions and anchor examples to enhance clarity and reproducibility. This comprehensive documentation ensures a transparent and systematic understanding of the research methodology.

(2) **Argumentative validation of interpretations** *("Argumentative Interpretationsabsicherung"):* Interpretations of the data were rigorously supported by logical arguments and empirical evidence. Each interpretation was grounded

in data from interviews and contextualized with relevant literature. This approach ensures that the findings are not only empirically grounded, but also logically coherent.

(3) **Proximity to the subject matter** *("Naehe zum Gegenstand"):* The research maintained a close and direct connection to the subject matter, emphasizing the real-world application and implications of blockchain-based bonds. This proximity was achieved by selecting experts who are actively involved in the field. Additionally, the use of semi-structured interviews facilitated an in-depth exploration of the topic, allowing for a comprehensive understanding that is closely aligned with practical realities.

(4) **Rule-based analysis** *("Regelgeleitetheit"):* The study adhered to a structured, rule-based approach in analyzing the interview data, following Mayring (2015)'s principles of qualitative content analyses. This systematic coding and categorization process, along with the use of code memos, ensured methodological consistency and reliability.

(5) **Communicative validation** *("Kommunikative Validierung"):* This process involved discussing key findings and interpretations with four interview participants. Their input allowed for the verification and refinement of the interpretations, thereby bolstering the study's credibility.

(6) **Triangulation** *("Triangulation"):* Data-source triangulation was accomplished through the integration and discussion of diverse perspectives and sources. This process included insights from expert interviews and an extensive review of related literature. Such an approach facilitated the cross-validation of findings and minimization of potential biases.

In conclusion, this study's adherence to Mayring (2016)'s quality criteria underpins a robust and reliable exploration of the impact of blockchain-based bonds on corporate financing and bond markets. The thorough procedural documentation, argumentative validation of interpretations, adherence to subject matter proximity, rule-based analysis, communicative validation, and the employment of triangulation collectively bolstered the methodological rigor and validity of the findings.

4 Data Analysis

This chapter provides a systematic analysis of the expert opinions on the impact of blockchain-based bonds on corporate financing and the bond market, structured around the four key research questions. It begins with comparing blockchain-based bonds and traditional bonds, emphasizing differences in accessibility, risk, cost, and transparency. Following this step, the analysis covers current trends as well as benefits and adoption barriers of blockchain-based bonds, highlighting their implications in the market. Moreover, the chapter explores the potential transformative effects of blockchain technology on the roles of market intermediaries and infrastructure providers in bond markets. It concludes with an assessment of expert opinions on the future trajectory of blockchain-based bonds, presenting insights into emerging trends and prospective developments.

4.1 Comparison With Traditional Bonds

This section provides a comparative analysis between blockchain-based bonds and traditional bonds, with a focus on accessibility, risk, cost, and transparency. Initially, it assesses whether blockchain technology can enhance market accessibility for both issuers and investors. The analysis then progresses to evaluating the risk profiles of both instruments, contrasting the various types of risk associated with each. Following this evaluation, the section explores the cost aspects, including issuance and trading expenses, to highlight potential process efficiencies offered by blockchain. Lastly, it examines the impact of blockchain technology

Supplementary Information The online version contains supplementary material available at https://doi.org/10.1007/978-3-658-45311-4_4.

M. M. Grossmann, *Blockchain-Based Bonds*, BestMasters,
https://doi.org/10.1007/978-3-658-45311-4_4

on the transparency of bond transactions, providing insights into how it may alter current practices. This structured approach was designed to yield a comprehensive understanding of blockchain's potential to transform the bond market.

4.1.1 Accessibility

Exploring the accessibility of blockchain-based bonds reveals various challenges and opportunities from the perspectives of issuers and investors.

4.1.1.1 Issuers

For issuers, blockchain-based bonds currently offer a lower level of market accessibility compared to traditional bonds. This restriction is particularly pronounced for larger companies with high issuance volumes, mainly due to a limited investor base equipped with the necessary infrastructure for purchasing blockchain-based bonds (Interview 7, Expert 7, para. 10). However, in the long term, blockchain-based solutions are deemed to offer substantial benefits: Expert 17 highlights the potential for continuous market access and enhanced risk management given blockchain-based bonds' lower issuance cost, moving away from the constraints of large, infrequent issuances (Interview 15, Expert 17, paras. 14–16). This reduction in cost might be particularly advantageous for small and medium-sized enterprises (SMEs) by enhancing their access to capital markets. Expert 6 observes that SMEs, particularly those that have never issued bonds before, seem to have recognized the potential. Referring to the BaFin's "Crypto securities according to eWpG" list (BaFin, 2023b), he underscores the high proportion of such companies engaged in completed blockchain-based transactions to date compared to larger institutions (Interview 6, Expert 6, para. 37).

4.1.1.2 Investors

Investors currently face challenges in accessing blockchain-based bonds, primarily because they are not available on mainstream trading platforms like XETRA (Interview 4, Expert 4, para. 29). They must adapt to new infrastructure requirements, including completing KYC processes and registering with specific blockchain custodians, which can be a time-consuming endeavor (Interview 14, Expert 17, para. 7). However, as these bonds gain traction, the obstacles are expected to diminish, leading to wider adoption and improved accessibility (Interview 7, Expert 7, para. 8). The tokenization aspect of blockchain-based bonds may be particularly promising for enhancing accessibility for retail investors, as it could allow for investments in smaller denominations (Interview 8, Expert 8, para. 8).

4.1.2 Risk

This section outlines expert comparisons between blockchain-based and traditional bonds, focusing on risks related to creditworthiness, liquidity, settlement, technology, and legal considerations.

4.1.2.1 Creditworthiness

Interviews with the study's experts indicate a consensus that the credit risk of blockchain-based bonds mirrors that of traditional bonds. This similarity is attributed to the unchanged fundamentals and issuer identity, regardless of the transaction method. For example, as Expert 7 points out, the risk associated with an issuer like Siemens remains constant whether the bond is issued through blockchain or traditional channels—summarized succinctly as "Siemens is Siemens, whether via blockchain or traditional means" (Interview 7, Expert 7, para. 6, translated by the author).

4.1.2.2 Liquidity

Liquidity risk significantly differentiates blockchain-based bonds from traditional bonds. Blockchain-based bonds face challenges in being listed on traditional exchanges, as they would need to be booked with a CSD. This issue undermines the benefits of blockchain technology (Interview 4, Expert 4, para. 21). Consequently, while traditional bonds benefit from consistent liquidity in established secondary markets, blockchain-based bonds typically rely on over-the-counter (OTC) settlements. That reliance, in turn, restricts their tradability and market appeal (Interview 10, Expert 10, paras. 20, 30).

Additionally, blockchain-based bonds not registered with a CSD are currently ineligible for European Central Bank (ECB) programs, meaning they cannot be used as collateral in ECB refinancing operations—a crucial factor for maintaining liquidity and financial stability, especially during economic downturns (Interview 2, Expert 2, para. 6).

This limited liquidity presents a significant hurdle, particularly for asset managers and institutional investors who require liquidity for operational flexibility as well as to comply with legally required liquidity ratios (Interview 4, Expert 4, para. 27). Consequently, investors often seek a premium to compensate for the heightened liquidity risks of blockchain-based bonds (Interview 13, Expert 15, para. 25).

In conclusion, blockchain-based bonds currently face significantly higher liquidity risks than traditional bonds. To enhance the viability and appeal of blockchain-based bonds, it is crucial to overcome these challenges. Key steps include establishing robust secondary markets and ensuring their eligibility for ECB programs.

4.1.2.3 Settlement

Experts widely acknowledge the potential of blockchain technology to minimize settlement risk in bond transactions. Blockchain facilitates P2P, DvP transactions in real time, known as atomic settlements. This capability effectively reduces the risk of default or delay (Interview 6, Expert 6, para. 37). However, the interviewees point out that current implementations have limitations: Current solutions for cash settlement on chain involving fiat currencies are not yet matured, leading the cash component to still depend on traditional banking channels (Interview 4, Expert 4, para. 65). This restriction sustains a degree of settlement risk and hinders the reduction of settlement periods from T + 5 ("trading day + 5 days") today to T + 0 (Interview 1, Expert 1, para. 23).

The integration of blockchain with suitable digital cash systems is viewed as crucial for fully harnessing its capabilities (Interview 10, Expert 10, para. 26). Experts debate the ideal design of on-chain cash solutions, with most favoring the implementation of wholesale CBDCs. As they are backed by central banks, CBDCs do not carry any inherent risks and are deemed the most efficient solution for on-chain cash settlements in fiat (Interview 3, Expert 3, para. 46). While stablecoins—which are pegged to an underlying fiat currency—are seen as effective interim solutions until a more robust wholesale CBDC system is established (Interview 11, Expert 12, para. 47), their long-term viability is questioned due to risks associated with their issuers (Interview 15, Expert 18, para. 76).

Some experts also consider alternatives such as Fnality—a digital payment system using tokenized fiat central bank deposits—as a practicable option alongside or in place of CBDCs, provided their reliability matches current bank money transactions (Interviews 5 and 15, Experts 5 and 19, paras. 38, 74).

In conclusion, blockchain-based bonds currently do not offer a significant advantage over traditional bonds in terms of settlement risks, as they rely on traditional banking channels for cash transactions. However, future integration with mature digital cash systems—which allow for fiat settlement in the broadest sense—is expected to bring transformative changes that could potentially reduce or eliminate settlement risks and enable more secure and efficient P2P financial transactions.

4.1.2.4 Technology

When evaluating the potential of blockchain-based bonds, understanding the technological risks in comparison to traditional bonds is crucial. Experts note that blockchain's decentralization—lacking a single governing entity for maintaining network stability—does not necessarily introduce more risk than traditional, centrally governed systems. This similarity is mainly because even central authorities like Clearstream might not fully mitigate damage in the event of a system failure (Interview 14, Expert 16, paras. 45–50). However, the novelty of blockchain technology leads Expert 4 to observe a slight uptick in operational risks in blockchain-based bonds (Interview 4, Expert 4, para. 65). Furthermore, Expert 7 underscores the need for comprehensive testing and integration of blockchain with existing systems, a process still in progress (Interview 7, Expert 7, para. 6).

However, there is growing consensus suggesting that the perceived technological risks may reduce over time. This expected decrease is attributed to the accumulation of experience and the evolution of standards. Expert 2 believes that, once blockchain platforms demonstrate consistent reliability in practical applications, the perceived technological risks will be comparable to traditional bonds. Moreover, he concludes that their impact on bond ratings is rather limited, pointing to the fact that, although issued on a blockchain, the digital bond of the European Investment Bank (EIB) received a rating similar to its traditional counterpart (Interview 2, Expert 2, para. 28).

In summary, blockchain-based bonds currently present a slightly higher technological risk compared to traditional bonds. The decentralized nature of blockchain is not inherently riskier, but emerging technologies generally bring risks that require further testing and integration. As the technology matures, these risks are expected to decrease. Nevertheless, the impact of current technological risks on bond ratings is deemed rather limited.

4.1.2.5 Legal Considerations

Experts commend the advanced legal framework surrounding blockchain-based bonds in Europe, notably in Germany with the eWpG. They highlight its progression compared to other jurisdictions like the U.S., especially its explicit recognition of securities issued on a blockchain as equivalent to traditional securities when certain conditions are met. This framework provides clear regulatory guidance for handling and registering securities on decentralized ledgers (Interview 3, Expert 3, para. 30).

The interviewees acknowledge the legal viability of blockchain-based bonds while also highlighting key regulatory challenges. These include the difficulties in trading fully decentralized securities on traditional exchanges and their ineligibility for ECB programs, as detailed in Section 4.1.2.2.

Additionally, experts point out the dynamic nature of the legal framework governing blockchain-based bonds. Despite a solid base of case law and existing legislation, new regulations like the eWpG introduce further complexities. Though promising, the new regulations have not been widely interpreted in judicial contexts, leading some interviewees to consider this context as a risk, albeit a modest one (Interview 7, Expert 7, para. 6).

In summary, Germany's legal framework, especially following the introduction of the eWpG, has generally aligned the legal risks of blockchain-based bonds with traditional bonds. However, this level of legal alignment is not yet widespread in other countries. In jurisdictions lacking such comprehensive and explicit regulations, blockchain-based bonds may face higher legal risks compared to their traditional counterparts.

4.1.3 Cost

The expert analysis on the cost comparison between traditional and blockchain-based bonds reveals a nuanced landscape with both shared perspectives and divergent views.

Key insights point to the high costs in the traditional bond market, mainly due to multiple intermediaries during issuance (Interview 3, Expert 3, para. 34), custody (Interview 10, Expert 10, para. 26), and trading (Interview 13, Expert 14, para. 27).

There is unanimous agreement among the study's experts on the potential of blockchain technology to reduce intermediary involvement and streamline processes, which could revolutionize the cost structure (Interview 4, Expert 4, para. 12). However, experts also advise caution at this stage: Due to the initial groundwork to be laid and the lack of standardized processes, the anticipated cost advantages of blockchain-based bond issuances are not yet realizable. In fact, current blockchain issuances may even be more expensive (Interview 5, Expert 5, para. 10–12).

The level of cost savings achievable will largely depend on the extent to which processes become ingrained and disintermediation is permitted by regulators (Interview 8, Expert 8, para. 40). As such, it is too early to accurately predict the savings (Interview 6, Expert 6, para. 31). Experts also express varied views on potential investor benefits beyond lower custody or transfer costs. This range of views includes uncertainties about whether issuers will pass on some of their cost savings to investors, possibly through higher coupon payments (Interview 4, Expert 4, para. 65; Interview 14, Expert 16, para. 41–43).

In summary, the expert insights depict a bond market at the dawn of a transformation. Traditional bonds are marked by high intermediary costs, a challenge that blockchain-based bonds aim to address. However, as blockchain application in bond markets is still nascent, it incurs high short-term transformation costs. Nevertheless, the long-term outlook is promising, with substantial cost reductions anticipated as blockchain technology matures and integrates more seamlessly into the financial landscape.

4.1.4 Transparency

In traditional bond issuances, issuers gain initial transparency into the investor base through the order book during the issuance. However, this visibility is limited to the early stage, and issuers lose sight of subsequent movements in the secondary market. They cannot track which investors might significantly reduce their holdings or which investors might substantially increase their positions (Interview 13, Expert 15, para. 32).

In contrast, blockchain technology maintains a complete, transparent transaction history accessible to all network participants, but under a pseudonymized wallet address. The interviewees highlight two scenarios in evaluating transparency: one where issuers have access to the real-world identities behind the wallet addresses via the registrar, and another where they do not.

When issuers have access to the real-world identities of investors, they gain a more comprehensive understanding of bond ownership. This understanding extends beyond the initial structure at the time of primary issuance. Experts suggest that this transparency enables issuers to engage with investors more strategically. They can leverage insights gained from trading volumes and market activities to enhance bond management and investor relations throughout the bond's lifecycle (Interview 13, Expert 15, para. 32). Yet, Expert 17 notes that the extent to which newly acquired information can be leveraged to advantage remains uncertain. This uncertainty is especially relevant considering that investor relations departments of issuers already maintain regular contact with major investors (Interview 15, Expert 17, para. 41).

Conversely, without access to real-world identities behind blockchain addresses, the scenario is markedly different. Although issuers can track the movement and ownership of bonds, their understanding of the investor base remains limited. The pseudonymization inherent in blockchain transactions limits the issuers' ability to tailor engagement strategies, as they cannot ascertain the true identities of their investors (Interview 15, Expert 18, para. 36).

In this context, the increased visibility does not necessarily yield actionable insights into investor behaviors or preferences, and thus does not profoundly influence issuer-investor dynamics (Interview 8, Expert 8, para. 28). As Expert 11 puts it: "So, now you may argue from an issuer perspective that the increased transparency and knowledge of who buys this, et cetera, is of interest, but only to the extent that you can actually monetize this information. If you can crystallize a benefit out of this information. If that's not the case, then it is not a sustainable business case" (Interview 11, Expert 12, para. 22).

Privacy concerns are paramount in both scenarios, particularly if the bond is issued on a public network. The transparent nature of blockchain technology raises confidentiality and data protection issues. For example, issuers may prefer not to disclose whether their issuance has been fully syndicated, and investors might wish to keep their investment strategies confidential (Interview 2, Expert 2, para. 44). The potential risk of de-anonymization, such as through pattern analyses, underscores the importance of developing advanced privacy solutions within blockchain systems (Interview 5, Expert 5, para. 43–44).

Also unaffected by the scenario is the capability of blockchains to offer detailed transparency about the underlying asset itself. For instance, it enables immutable documentation and sharing of the intended use of the bond proceeds. Expert 13 emphasizes that this transparency fosters a higher level of accountability that is typically rewarded by the market and is especially advantageous in the context of the EU taxonomy (Interview 12, Expert 13, paras. 34–36).

In summary, blockchain enhances transparency across the bond lifecycle, offering a detailed transaction history. However, its benefits vary: They are more significant when issuers can identify real-world investor identities, enabling better engagement with investors. Without this link, however, the increased transparency provides limited insights. Privacy concerns, especially in public networks, underscore the need for advanced privacy solutions in blockchain. Additionally, the detailed transparency about underlying assets, such as the usage of the bond proceeds, is particularly valued in contexts like the EU taxonomy.

4.2 Benefits, Barriers, and Market-Adoption Dynamics

This chapter investigates the benefits and challenges associated with blockchain-based bonds, along with their current patterns of adoption in the market. It begins by presenting expert perspectives on blockchain's transformative potential in the bond market. The chapter then systematically analyzes the barriers to widespread adoption, applying the "Technology—Organization—Environment" framework from Section 2.2.9. The analysis concludes with a detailed examination of the prevailing market adoption trends, incorporating expert views on the DLT Pilot Regime. This approach aims to provide an in-depth exploration of the market perception around blockchain-based bonds.

4.2.1 Benefits

Expert insights suggest that blockchain technology is highly valued for its potential transformative impact on the bond sector. Four key improvements are particularly emphasized.

Firstly, experts underscore blockchain's ability to significantly shorten settlement times. Traditional settlement periods, such as T + 5, could be reduced to nearly instantaneous transactions that are executable 24/7. This feature is particularly beneficial for large-scale institutional transactions where timing is critical to financial outcomes (Interview 3, Expert 3, para. 22). Such an improvement could not only reduce settlement risk, as discussed in Section 4.1.2.3, but also enhance capital efficiency by freeing up funds and assets more quickly (Interview 10, Expert 10, para. 44). Considering the global trend toward faster settlement standards, such as the T + 1 initiative already underway in the U.S., blockchain is set to play a critical role in supporting robust regulatory compliance (Interview 7, Expert 7, para. 28).

Secondly, blockchain has the potential to redefine the concept of a "single source of truth" in finance. Its immutable ledger combines bond settlement and delivery into a unified system, reducing the need for multiple databases and separate systems. This integration ensures data consistency in back-office operations, such as risk control and accounting, and can help resolve internal discrepancies within corporations regarding data accuracy. Such consolidation could significantly increase organizational efficiency (Interview 1, Expert 1, paras. 23–25).

Thirdly, experts recognize smart contracts as a key innovation in blockchain that substantially enhances operational efficiency and compliance in the bond sector. Smart contracts allow precise control of transaction timing and sequencing, leading to full automation and scalable funding (Interview 3, Expert 3, para. 22). They also support critical security and legal requirements, like ensuring that transactions occur only between authorized addresses (Interview 4, Expert 4, para. 43). Additionally, they can streamline processes—for instance, by pre-validating transaction steps (Interview 11, Expert 11, para. 15), or by replacing traditional paper documentation (Interview 3, Expert 3, para. 12).

Lastly, experts have high regard for blockchain's versatility, especially with a view to its capacity to manage diverse financial processes beyond just bonds. Its open architecture allows for a unified platform accommodating various financial instruments, such as securities, derivatives, and swaps, thereby enabling innovative financial solutions (Interview 3, Expert 3, para. 26). Expert 1 suggests that blockchain's integration in the bond market might spur its adoption for other asset classes like cash, equities, and derivatives, potentially leading to a common ledger for managing all these components (Interview 1, Expert 1, para. 49).

In summary, experts suggest that blockchain-based solutions could significantly transform bond markets. They emphasize the technology's capacity to facilitate faster transaction settlements, maintain data integrity, automate processes through smart contracts, and encourage the development of innovative solutions. The incorporation of blockchain into the bond market may serve as a catalyst for its broader application across various financial instruments, possibly signaling a shift toward a more efficient financial ecosystem.

4.2.2 Barriers

The subsequent section will explore the challenges faced by blockchain-based bonds that impede their widespread adoption. These findings will be organized within the "Technology—Organization—Environment" framework, as proposed by Tornatzky et al. (1990), mirroring the structure employed in Section 2.2.9.

4.2.2.1 Technological Barriers

From a technological standpoint, discussions with experts highlighted two primary issues: First, the fragmentation and lack of interoperability within the blockchain ecosystem; and second, the limited transaction throughput, which restricts the number of transactions blockchains can process per second.

There is a consensus among the study's experts that fragmentation and interoperability shortfalls significantly hamper the scalability of blockchain-based bonds (Interview 2, Expert 2, para. 8). Activities like issuing, repurchasing, or settling bonds require connections with various platforms and networks to maximize investor access and demand. Achieving such interoperability is crucial for market growth and broader technology adoption (Interview 15, Expert 18, para. 49). However, Expert 10 emphasizes that it is important to take one step at a time. He advocates for the general establishment of secondary markets within specific networks before addressing cross-system interoperability (Interview 10, Expert 10, para. 21–22).

The market is currently subject to considerable fragmentation across blockchain initiatives (Interview 2, Expert 2, para. 8). While blockchain has the potential to set global standards, especially in cross-border transactions, addressing fragmentation is essential to unlock this potential (Interview 7, Expert 7, para. 26). Establishing effective interoperability requires a collaborative effort between banks and investors to agree on a common standard for protocols. Without this commitment, achieving interoperability and scalability will remain challenging (Interview 3, Expert 3, para. 24).

The transaction throughput of blockchain networks has emerged as another focal point. However, given that bond trading does not typically match the frequency of daily retail transactions, experts concur that the throughput capabilities of existing blockchain solutions, such as Ethereum's sidechain Polygon, suffice for existing needs (Interview 10, Expert 10, para. 14). Nevertheless, anticipating evolving market demands, Expert 4 emphasizes the importance of continuously optimizing and developing solutions for future scalability (Interview 4, Expert 4, para. 45).

Reflecting on these considerations, Expert 2 states: "Given the current market volume today, I think that what Ethereum brings as transactions per second is enough. But for the future: You have the second-layer options. I think that once we have clear use cases, to optimize, find technical, new solutions, it will go pretty fast. But first we have to 'pay' those engineers with a business, and we have to generate business before that. I am pretty confident that we will find adequate solutions when the business will be there. We cannot use the scalability problem as an excuse not for doing innovation in the blockchain space" (Interview 2, Expert 2, para. 12).

In summary, addressing key technological challenges such as the fragmentation and lack of interoperability within the blockchain ecosystem, as well as improving transaction throughput, is vital for the scalability of blockchain-based bonds. Effectively overcoming these technological barriers is fundamental to achieving broader adoption of the technology.

4.2.2.2 Organizational Barriers

Interviewed experts also highlight organizational challenges in scaling blockchain-based bonds. They particularly emphasize the complexities in managing liquidity within organizations and the need for large investments in infrastructure. Moreover, experts conversely discuss the influence of workforce expertise on scalability.

Interviewees point out that, in today's financial environment, the shift toward atomic settlements could present considerable liquidity management challenges, especially for issuers. The core problem stems from unsynchronized transaction stages: Immediate settlement of outflows, such as coupon payments, contrasts with potential delays in inflows from traditional channels, potentially leading to internal liquidity shortfalls (Interview 11, Expert 11, para. 13). To effectively mitigate this discrepancy, issuers might need to maintain larger liquidity reserves, which could compromise the efficiency benefits of real-time settlements (Interview 11, Expert 12, para. 16). Moreover, linked hedging processes would need to be adapted to ensure that they continue to mesh seamlessly, which involves time and effort (Interview 14, Expert 16, para. 65). Hence, it can be concluded that, as long as most of the transaction volume within a company is processed via traditional channels, scalability on the issuer side remains limited.

Furthermore, establishing the necessary infrastructure for blockchain-based bonds, such as ensuring compatibility with existing systems, requires large investments. The need for demonstrable success to justify ongoing expenditures often slows down the adoption process (Interview 11, Expert 11, para. 29). This challenge is particularly acute for smaller banks, which may be hesitant to commit substantial resources without timely returns guaranteed (Interview 1, Expert 1, para. 7). Therefore, accurately assessing realizable efficiency gains would support the future scalability of blockchain-based bonds (Interview 7, Expert 7, para. 26).

The experts generally concur that there is a notable shortage of skilled personnel around blockchain technology within the market. Many emphasize a significant gap, particularly in roles that require a combination of blockchain expertise and financial market knowledge (Interview 13, Expert 14, para. 46). Most experts believe, however, that the necessary blockchain skills can be developed internally within organizations if decision-makers support the corresponding efforts (Interview 5, Expert 5, para. 48). Consequently, Expert 13 points to the lack of sufficient blockchain expertise among management board members. She considers this deficiency a critical obstacle to widespread implementation (Interview 12, Expert 13, para. 54).

In summary, scaling blockchain-based bonds faces organizational challenges, notably in managing liquidity due to the shift toward atomic settlements and to the large investments required for infrastructure. While there is a noticeable shortage of skilled blockchain personnel, experts believe that these skills can be developed internally. Nonetheless, the insufficient blockchain expertise among board members is identified as a critical barrier to the broader implementation of blockchain-based bonds.

4.2.2.3 Environmental Barriers

Within the category "Environmental," experts highlight several factors that impede the growth of blockchain-based bonds. These include liquidity constraints, the lack of integrated on-chain cash settlement, and legal fragmentation within the blockchain ecosystem.

A key barrier to the widespread adoption of blockchain-based bonds is their limited liquidity. This issue arises from challenges such as difficulties in obtaining stock-exchange listings, non-compliance with ECB eligibility criteria if not registered with a CSD, and the absence of robust secondary markets, as elaborated in Section 4.1.2.2. Strict liquidity ratio requirements imposed on institutional investors further constrain the market appeal and growth potential of these bonds.

Expert 1 succinctly summarizes this situation: "So, when you issue a [blockchain-based] bond, it's a buy-and-hold kind of strategy. So, I can issue it, I can sell it to some investors, and there's no liquidity behind, there's no market where I can go and trade it. They're not listed on an exchange. And so, it's kind of limiting. We can't build a big business on that basically" (Interview 1, Expert 1, para. 5). As such, it can be concluded that these liquidity constraints are not mere inconveniences, but rather pivotal barriers impeding the scalability of blockchain-based bonds.

Furthermore, while blockchain technology can theoretically facilitate secure and efficient transaction settlements, the lack of mature on-chain cash settlement-systems involving fiat currencies currently hampers this potential. This issue is explored in more detail in Section 4.1.2.3. Experts identify this shortfall as a significant barrier to scalability that prevent full realization of blockchain's advantages in the bond market (Interview 14, Expert 16, paras. 20–21).

In addition, addressing regulatory fragmentation across different jurisdictions is highlighted as crucial, especially for issuers handling large financing volumes and seeking broad market access. Experts suggest that establishing harmonized legal frameworks that uniformly reflect the particularities of the technology is essential for making blockchain-based bonds a scalable option (Interview 15, Expert 18, para. 49).

In summary, addressing the outlined "environmental" challenges is critical for the scalability of blockchain-based bonds. These challenges include overcoming liquidity constraints, integrating suitable on-chain cash settlements involving fiat currencies, and resolving legal fragmentation within the blockchain ecosystem. Tackling these barriers is vital for fostering a more efficient blockchain environment in financial markets, which in turn is essential for broader adoption of these instruments.

4.2.3 Market-Adoption Dynamics

This section begins with an overview of the current market-adoption dynamics of blockchain-based bonds. It then delves into the specific impacts of the EU's DLT Pilot Regime, drawing on expert insights to understand its advancements and limitations.

4.2.3.1 General

Experts acknowledge the theoretical potential of blockchain in bond markets, but substantial challenges currently restrict its adoption to a nascent stage (Interview 7, Expert 7, para. 4). Interestingly, there is a notable difference in the level of commitment to exploring blockchain-based bonds between organizations, particularly when comparing bond issuers and transaction facilitators.

Transaction facilitators identify two main drivers for their interest in blockchain-based bonds: understanding and leveraging the technology's theoretical benefits, as well as a strong concern about missing out on crucial technological advancements. Expert 8 likens this uneasiness to the fear of a "Kodak moment," where waiting for absolute certainty about the efficiency gains this technology could bring, might be a strategic misstep (Interview 8, Expert 8, para. 18). Expert 14 emphasizes the anticipated momentum in implementing blockchain technology, arguing that early exploration is strategically essential to avoid being left behind (Interview 13, Expert 14, para. 34).

These drivers have led numerous traditional financial institutions to actively explore and progress in the field of blockchain-based bonds, including obtaining necessary licenses (Interview 6, Expert 6, para. 6). In addition, fintech companies, specializing in unlocking blockchain's potential, are well-positioned to capitalize on this trend (Interview 12, Expert 13, para. 10).

From the perspective of issuers, the approach to blockchain-based bonds is more reserved. Expert 16 reports that its corporation adopts a "wait-and-see" approach, emphasizing the need to balance technological progress with financial considerations (Interview 14, Expert 16, para. 4). In a similar vein, Expert 18 shares that the blockchain-based bond transaction executed by its corporation was driven more by curiosity and the desire for experience than by immediate financial benefits. They sought to test the waters and understand how decentralized placements function, preparing for future opportunities that blockchain technology might present (Interview 15, Expert 18, para. 45). Consequently, blockchain-based bonds have not yet substantially influenced their refinancing strategies (Interview 15, Expert 18, para. 78).

Furthermore, considering market demand is crucial when assessing the trajectory of blockchain-based bonds. Interviewees agree that investor demand significantly influences their pace of adoption (Interview 3, Expert 3, para. 16). For this reason, Expert 13 highlights that the expansion of blockchain-based issuances depends on attracting customers who recognize and actively seek the technology's efficiency benefits (Interview 12, Expert 13, para. 58). The expert notes the current investor demand is relatively low, likening it to "a chicken and egg situation," in which more institutions offering these bonds may stimulate increased investor interest, and vice versa (Interview 12, Expert 13, para. 30).

Moreover, trust in the technology is highlighted as another key determinant of investor demand. Negative perceptions, often fueled by headlines related to areas like cryptocurrencies, can dissuade entities from issuing or purchasing blockchain-based bonds (Interview 15, Expert 19, paras. 69–70).

In summary, blockchain-based bonds are in an early, exploratory stage with differing levels of engagement. Transaction facilitators with fintechs and traditional financial institutions alike are keenly exploring the technology, driven by its potential and by a fear of falling behind in technological advancements. Issuers, however, are more reserved, focusing on balancing technological progress with financial considerations. Investor demand is a crucial factor for the pace of adoption, intertwined with supply and trust in the technology. Hence, despite its innovative potential, the impact of blockchain on mainstream financial strategies currently remains limited.

4.2.3.2 Impact of DLT Pilot Regime

The EU's DLT Pilot Regime was initiated to evaluate the integration of blockchain technology in financial markets within a controlled, sandboxed environment. As such, it aims to explore the potential and limitations of blockchain-based bonds. Although it has made strides in introducing secondary market capabilities, expert opinions predominantly suggest its impact on the broader adoption of blockchain in bond issuance remains limited.

A few interviewees express profound skepticism toward the DLT Pilot Regime, with Expert 9 notably labeling it as "mostly marketing" (Interview 9, Expert 9, para. 24). Yet, in principle, most experts acknowledge its significant contribution, particularly in introducing secondary-market capabilities for blockchain-based bonds (Interview 6, Expert 6, para. 25). Moreover, they commend the DLT Pilot Regime for enhancing collaboration and information exchange between banks and regulators, recognizing this as a vital step in creating a conducive market environment (Interview 6, Expert 6, para. 41).

However, concerns are raised about the Regime's volume restrictions and its temporary nature, along with uncertainty over its future incorporation into permanent law. Several experts argue that these limitations may act as barriers to substantial engagement, potentially leading to unamortized expenses and limited participation (Interview 4, Expert 4, para. 31). Yet, some experts understand that such prudence is essential to avoid jeopardizing financial stability, even as they acknowledge the limitations it imposes (Interview 2, Expert 2, para. 18).

Expert 4 specifically critiques the six-year duration of the sandbox regime as too long, arguing that it may hinder real business growth beyond experimental settings. Additionally, he considers the volume restrictions as overly limiting, potentially diminishing the economic appeal in a wider market context. These constraints may hinder the broader adoption and popularity of blockchain technology in the bond market (Interview 4, Expert 4, para. 77).

Despite these challenges, several experts emphasize the value of gaining hands-on experience with blockchain-based bonds during, but not limited to, the Regime to positively influence future regulatory changes. They recommend proactive collaboration and engagement, stressing the need to share insights that could guide regulatory adjustments and enhancements. Such involvement is considered crucial for advancing the widespread implementation of digital securities (Interview 6, Expert 6, para. 39).

In summary, the DLT Pilot Regime is pivotal for blockchain's integration in bond issuances but faces challenges. Its contributions to secondary-market capabilities and regulatory collaboration are noted, but its volume restrictions and temporary status raise concerns about its long-term impact on market adoption. Experts suggest using insights gained during the Regime to inform future regulatory enhancements, highlighting its potential role in advancing blockchain in the bond market.

4.3 Transformation of Intermediary and Infrastructure-Provider Roles

This chapter explores the potential transformative impact of blockchain technology on the roles and functions of market intermediaries and infrastructure providers in bond markets. It begins with a broad assessment, then delves into specific role transformations. This includes examining how traditional entities, such as investment banks, clearinghouses, CSDs, and custodian banks, would adapt to a blockchain-centric environment. The chapter also investigates the emergence of new roles, like those of crypto registrars and platform providers, examining their integration into this evolving landscape. Through this analysis, the chapter presents a comprehensive overview of how blockchain technology is reshaping the dynamics of financial market intermediation.

4.3.1 Overall Assessment

In the evolving landscape of blockchain-based bonds, there is a consensus among the interviewed experts on the potential transformative impact on market infrastructure and the roles of intermediaries. While blockchain is recognized for its ability to enhance market efficiency, intermediaries are expected to play a crucial role, particularly in the early stages of adoption (Interview 5, Expert 5, para. 22).

Under the eWpG framework, the only legally mandated intermediary role is that of the registrar. In the simplest scenario, this framework leads to a structure consisting only of the issuer, registrar, and investor (refer to Fig. 4.1). However, currently, seeking a listing on a traditional exchange would additionally require central registration with a CSD, as detailed in Section 4.1.2.2.

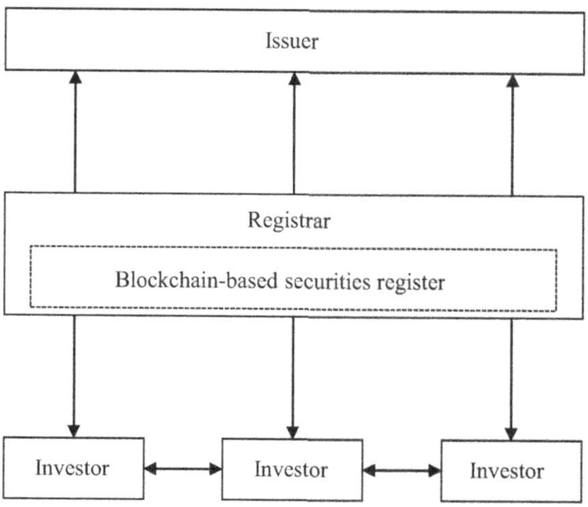

Fig. 4.1 Leanest Setup Possible in a Blockchain-Based Bond Transaction Under eWpG. (Source: Own illustration)

Nonetheless, the experts anticipate a continuingly significant role for intermediaries in facilitating market access, providing wallet solutions, and offering technical support. They also predict that not just traditional intermediaries, but also smaller, specialized firms will emerge to provide these services. This shift is expected to stimulate competition, potentially leading to more competitive pricing, and spurring innovation (Interview 6, Expert 6, para. 10). The future extent of disintermediation will largely depend on how issuers and investors will assess the cost-benefit ratio of these intermediary services (Interview 3, Expert 3, para. 42).

In summary, while blockchain-based bonds are set to alter market infrastructure and increase efficiency, the intermediary role is anticipated to evolve with the market. As blockchain becomes more prevalent in the bond market, intermediaries are likely to adapt, focusing on specialized, value-adding services.

4.3.2 Specific Role Transformations

As outlined, broad adoption of blockchain technology in the financial landscape would drive significant transformation, characterized by the emergence of new roles, the adaptation of existing ones, and the potential elimination of others. The forthcoming sections will delve into the new roles brought about by blockchain technology, with a specific focus on crypto registrars, platform providers, and network providers. Subsequently, the discussion will examine how traditional entities, including investment banks, clearinghouses, CSDs, and custodian banks, are expected to adapt in this environment. Supporting roles, such as information intermediaries or providers of tokenization solutions, are not included for reasons of simplicity.

4.3.2.1 New Roles

The subsequent sections present expert opinions on the emerging roles in a blockchain-based bond market, focusing on crypto registrars, platform providers, and network providers.

4.3.2.1.1 Crypto Registrars

In blockchain-based bond issuances under the eWpG, crypto registrars, licensed by the BaFin, assume a critical, legally mandated role. Their main responsibilities include maintaining accurate token ownership records, ensuring the technical functionality of blockchain transactions, and overseeing legal compliance. Although issuers have the option of taking on the registrar role by themselves, the expert consensus is that this function is best managed by specialized intermediaries. Utilizing the expertise and capabilities of these intermediaries is deemed more effective and reliable for handling the complexities of blockchain transactions and maintaining adherence to regulatory standards (Interview 15, Expert 18, paras. 24–26).

4.3.2.1.2 Platform Providers

While blockchain technology greatly enhances the bond-settlement process, it alone cannot bridge the gap between supply and demand. Experts agree that there is a need for an institution to establish and manage infrastructure for secondary-market trading, effectively matching supply with demand while ensuring regulatory compliance (Interview 8, Expert 8, para. 12). Additionally, Expert 17 suggests that issuers could leverage these platforms to sell bonds directly through auction processes (Interview 14, Expert 17, para. 17). Banks, with their established reputation, are considered well-suited for this role, although other entities could also fulfill these responsibilities (Interview 4, Expert 4, para. 27).

4.3.2.1.3 Network Providers

In the scenario of a private blockchain solution, an institution would be needed to establish and maintain the corresponding network (Interview 2, Expert 2, para. 2). If a public blockchain infrastructure is utilized, this role becomes unnecessary, as a public network serves as a common good (Interview 12, Expert 13, para. 12).

4.3.2.2 Traditional Intermediaries

This section explores expert assessments regarding the changing roles of traditional financial intermediaries in a blockchain-based bond market, emphasizing investment banks, clearinghouses, CSDs, and custodian banks.

4.3.2.2.1 Investment Banks

Experts identify two primary roles for investment banks in blockchain-based bond issuances: ensuring compliance as well as facilitating market access.

In ensuring compliance in a blockchain-based bond setup, investment banks' critical role, particularly in managing the complexities of the KYC process, is still universally recognized. Their expertise in regulatory requirements spares issuers and investors from conducting separate KYC processes, a dual approach deemed inefficient and potentially disadvantageous. Without banks as intermediaries, each party would face the need to share sensitive information that is typically protected under banking secrecy (Interview 14, Expert 16, para. 31). Additionally, the idea of shifting these responsibilities away from banks is viewed as impractical, given the technical and bureaucratic challenges inherent in financial transactions. These include, for example, checking the identities of the persons responsible for trading (Interview 7, Expert 7, para. 32).

Opinions vary regarding the role of banks in facilitating market access. Some experts emphasize their continued importance, especially in large benchmark issuances. They argue that, despite blockchain advancements, the nuanced processes of banks in outreach, investor selection, and book building are still vital (Interview 6, Expert 6, para. 12). Banks' ability to aggregate individual investor feedback into a comprehensive market perspective is critical to pricing decisions—a task that issuers may find challenging to replicate by themselves (Interview 14, Expert 16, para. 14). Furthermore, Expert 7 notes the role of banks in occasionally "topping up" to the planned issuance when the volume cannot be fully placed on the market (Interview 7, Expert 7, para. 32).

Conversely, other experts foresee a reduced role for banks, as blockchain enables more direct issuer-investor interactions, which challenges traditional banking intermediation (Interview 12, Expert 13, para. 42). This trend, however, may be more pronounced with large, well-established issuers. Experts outline that, especially for smaller companies and companies that are less active in the market, banks are still considered crucial in providing advisory services (Interview 15, Expert 17, para. 32). Their expertise in structuring transactions, determining pricing, and managing placements is deemed particularly valuable for entities lacking the necessary resources or in-house expertise. In this context, smaller entities tend to be more reliant on banks, unlike their larger, more market-active counterparts who may exhibit a reduced dependence (Interview 14, Expert 16, para. 27).

In summary, investment banks are considered to retain a crucial role in blockchain-based bond issuance, especially in ensuring compliance. While their role in market access may change with blockchain altering some functions, their importance in advisory services persists, especially for smaller or less experienced issuers. Overall, blockchain technology not only modifies some traditional functions of banks but also highlights their evolving roles as specialized advisors and supporters in the bond issuance process.

4.3.2.2.2 Clearinghouses

Experts present diverging views on the future role of clearinghouses, yet they converge on certain key aspects. There is a consensus that blockchain technology, especially by leveraging smart contracts, can automate many tasks traditionally performed by clearinghouses. These functions include executing transactions based on specific conditions like DvP (Interview 6, Expert 6, para. 12). This innovation suggests a shift away from conventional processes and questions the ongoing need for traditional clearinghouse organizations.

As for the future of clearinghouses, experts' opinions differ. The majority of the interviewees believes that blockchain, with its capacity for atomic settlements, might render these organizations obsolete by ensuring that transactions are either fully executed or not executed at all (Interview 2, Expert 2, para. 18). Yet, others envision clearinghouses adapting to new roles within a blockchain-based financial system, possibly functioning as coordinators or administrators who set rules to ensure financial system stability (Interview 1, Expert 1, para. 25).

However, experts collectively agree that, during the transition phase in which blockchain-based bonds and cash transactions are not yet fully integrated, clearinghouses will continue to be important (Interview 4, Expert 4, para. 17).

In summary, while there is consensus about blockchain's impact on clearinghouse functions, experts are split on whether these developments will lead to the organizations' complete elimination or to an evolution of their roles.

4.3.2.2.3 Central Securities Depositories

Many experts envision blockchain having the potential to fully eliminate traditional CSDs like Clearstream (Interview 8, Expert 8, para. 10). Similar to clearinghouses, Expert 1 suggests that CSDs might adapt by taking on new roles such as rule setting (Interview 1, Expert 1, para. 27).

However, the current legal framework, which mandates central registration of securities with CSDs for exchange listing, ensures their continued importance in the short term. This situation might evolve if regulations are amended to accommodate the listing of decentralized securities, potentially disrupting the current dominance of CSDs (Interview 4, Expert 4, para. 21). Nonetheless, Expert 2 underlines the critical role of CSDs in maintaining financial stability, advocating for a cautious approach to regulatory changes: "You cannot touch it without being very careful" (Interview 2, Expert 2, para. 18).

In response to the growing influence of blockchain, traditional CSDs like Clearstream, Euroclear, and DTCC are exploring strategies to adapt. These include initiatives to collaborate in creating a global ledger that integrates with their existing systems, similar to what blockchain technology could provide. Their approach aims to align with evolving market trends while preserving their established business models. As Expert 2 suggests: "Maybe the solution will be the three CSD connecting together, which is the global ledger, and there is no need for blockchain. But you see, then we have already won something as blockchain enthusiasts" (Interview 2, Expert 2, para. 20).

In conclusion, there is a consensus on the disruptive potential of blockchain concerning the traditional roles of CSDs. The extent and speed of this transformation, however, will depend on regulatory changes and market reactions. Moreover, the market's reception of alternative solutions will play a pivotal role in shaping the future trajectory.

4.3.2.2.4 Custodian Banks

In the evolving context of blockchain-based bonds, custodian banks are increasingly recognized for their potential role as crypto custodians. This development aligns with the growing preference for centralized, streamlined services, particularly considering complexities associated with managing digital assets across different blockchain networks. Despite blockchain's self-custody capabilities, especially private investors will continue to favor the user-friendly interfaces and established trust offered by custodian banks, notably in areas like tax compliance (Interview 3, Expert 3, para. 36–40).

Experts observe that banks are adapting by developing key management solutions and digital vaults to securely store a range of digital assets for clients, including bonds, digital deposits, NFTs, and others. To offer these crypto custody services in Germany, a BaFin license is necessary. Many banks are currently pursuing this accreditation (Interview 1, Expert 1, para. 47).

The role of custodian banks as crypto custodians extends beyond mere safekeeping; it encompasses asset servicing as well. Experts outline that—while blockchain allows for some operations, like coupon payments, to be automated through smart contracts—the custodian's involvement in governance remains crucial (Interview 9, Expert 9, para. 28–30).

In summary, as blockchain technology transforms the bond market, the role of custodian banks is evolving rather than diminishing. Their continued relevance—despite the self-custody options blockchain offers—is attributed to the complexities of digital asset management and to additional responsibilities like tax compliance in self-custody scenarios.

4.4 Outlook

This chapter offers a deep dive into expert opinions on the future of blockchain-based bonds, focusing on two key aspects: standards and overall prospects. It begins with an exploration of the importance of standardization, delving into the debate between the adoption of private versus public networks, while considering regulatory, technological, and market implications. The narrative then transitions to assessing the potential impact of blockchain-based bonds, contemplating whether they will revolutionize the bond market or coexist with traditional bonds. Additionally, the chapter acknowledges alternative, centralized approaches to bond digitalization, such as those represented by initiatives like D7.

4.4.1 Standards

In the rapidly evolving domain of blockchain-based bonds, the issue of standardization stands out as a key theme, as detailed in Section 4.2.2.1. The majority of experts underscore the need for industry-wide standards, considering them essential for ensuring efficiency and interoperability within the blockchain-based bond environment. Such requirements include the need for market participants to commit to specific platforms or protocols to facilitate progress (Interview 3, Expert 3, para. 24). One pivotal discussion point is the choice between private and public networks, with experts weighing the implications of each in terms of regulatory compliance, technological capabilities, and market dynamics.

Expert opinions are divided on network preferences. Many experts lean toward private networks, influenced by current regulatory trends and frameworks. According to Expert 13, the BCBS's recent recommendations, which show a preference for private over public blockchains, reinforce this regulatory inclination (Interview 12, Expert 13, para. 22). Experts also appreciate the superior control (Interview 13, Expert 14, para. 38) and the clear governance structure that private networks provide (Interview 6, Expert 6, para. 14).

Conversely, other experts support public blockchains, highlighting their scalability and the benefits of community-driven development (Interview 9, Expert 9, para. 10). Public networks, viewed as public goods, minimize the need for individual entities to maintain infrastructure (Interview 10, Expert 10, para. 10). The widespread adoption of the EVM and its role in enabling network interoperability is seen as a significant advantage of public blockchains (Interview 9, Expert 9, para. 10). Despite acknowledging challenges like higher transaction costs, the experts value the broad market access that public networks offer (Interview 2, Expert 2, para. 2).

To meet compliance standards, experts suggest that whitelisting wallets on public networks can be as effective as access-control mechanisms on private networks (Interview 4, Expert 4, para. 41). The opinions regarding the consensus mechanism to be used in the corresponding public network are uniform: Given their energy efficiency while maintaining robust security, PoS networks are preferred (Interview 10, Expert 10, para. 16).

In summary, expert perspectives highlight the intricacies of the blockchain-based bond landscape, influenced by technological advancements, regulatory frameworks, and market dynamics. First and foremost, regulatory developments—particularly the implementation of the BCBS recommendations—will significantly influence the evolution of this landscape and the convergence toward either private or public networks.

4.4.2 Prospects

The potential for blockchain-based bonds to replace traditional bonds generates a wide spectrum of expert opinions. Experts collectively acknowledge the transformative power of blockchain technology but agree that any significant shift toward its widespread adoption in the bond market would be gradual and shaped by various factors (Interview 5, Expert 5, para. 36). Key factors influencing this transition include technological developments, the establishment of industry standards, and overcoming current challenges (Interview 13, Expert 14, para. 48). Notably, the growing investment in blockchain projects by major banks reflects a strong, active interest in this field (Interview 6, Expert 6, para. 49).

The distribution of opinions among experts as to whether blockchain-based bonds have the potential to replace traditional bonds in the long term is balanced. Some experts are convinced that blockchain-based bonds will replace traditional instruments at a specific point in time, however, not in the near future (Interview 1, Expert 1, para. 35); others argue that the established processes of traditional bonds are too entrenched to be disrupted (Interview 7, Expert 7, para. 34). Building on that, Expert 2 notes: "If we really aim to disrupt the bond market and replace the existing system, we need more than just 5 to 10% improvement in cost or revenue. Nothing will change if we have only minimal improvements" (Interview 2, Expert 2, para. 14).

However, many experts who are skeptical about blockchain-based bonds entirely replacing traditional ones recognize their potential as valuable complements. They see blockchain as particularly beneficial in areas like environmental, social, and governance (ESG) funding, where it can enhance transparency in fund usage (Interview 2, Expert 2, para. 32).

The discussion also includes other digital, non-blockchain methods for transforming bond issuances. For example, Expert 7 mentions D7, a centralized solution that digitizes bonds through dematerialization, replacing physical certificates with electronic records (Interview 7, Expert 7, para. 4). This method aligns with frameworks like eWpG and shows the market's readiness to experiment with various technologies besides blockchain for improved efficiency in bond trading and settlement processes.

D7 demonstrates how electronic securities can retain a traditional "look and feel" and market depth for investors, as they are registered centrally and can be traded on traditional exchanges (Interview 13, Expert 15, para. 23). This complements Expert 18's viewpoint, emphasizing that blockchain's role in transforming the bond market is not yet set. He underscores that the solution providing the best cost-benefit ratio will likely dominate in the long run (Interview 15, Expert 18, para. 71).

In summary, this chapter presented a diverse range of perspectives on the future of blockchain in bond markets. It explored scenarios ranging from blockchain-based bonds replacing traditional ones to such bonds serving as complementary solutions, or being overshadowed by other non-blockchain digital solutions that offer better cost-benefit outcomes. The varied opinions reflect the complexity of evolving financial technologies and market trends. These differences in opinions underscore the importance of detailed knowledge of both technology and financial markets in shaping efficient bond markets.

Discussion

5

The following chapter synthesizes the insights from 19 industry experts across banking, fintech, corporate finance, and asset management to answer the subordinate research questions with a focused lens on the German market. This approach enables a differentiated answer to the main research question. Furthermore, the results are discussed and contextualized within the current body of literature. This approach aims to bridge the gap between theoretical concepts and practical insights from the field.

5.1 Comparison With Traditional Bonds

The first subordinate research question—"How do blockchain-based bonds compare to traditional bonds in terms of accessibility, risk, cost, and transparency?"—delves into the fundamental differences between these two types of bonds. This comparison is crucial for understanding how blockchain technology could revolutionize or disrupt the bond market. Table 5.1 succinctly compares blockchain-based bonds with traditional bonds from the perspective of the former, with a detailed analysis following in the subsequent section.

Blockchain-based bonds currently pose accessibility challenges for issuers and investors. Issuers face lower market accessibility compared to traditional bonds due to a limited investor base that has established the necessary infrastructure. However, in the long-term, these bonds may offer benefits such as continuous market access and lower issuance costs, with the latter particularly advantageous for SMEs. These results find support in the work of scholars like Popescu (2020), who underscore blockchain's capacity to democratize access to financial products, given its 24/7 availability and inherent cost efficiencies.

M. M. Grossmann, *Blockchain-Based Bonds*, BestMasters,
https://doi.org/10.1007/978-3-658-45311-4_5

Table 5.1 Blockchain-Based Bonds Versus Traditional Bonds

	Current Setup	Future Potential
Accessibility	Lower	Higher
Risk	Credit, settlement, and legal risks comparable; liquidity and technological risks higher	Credit, technological and legal risks comparable; settlement and liquidity risks lower
Cost	Lower operational cost, offset by large setup cost	Lower operational cost, large setup cost amortized
Transparency	Higher, but only beneficial if real identities are known	Higher, but only beneficial if real identities are known

Note: The comparison is based on the perspective of blockchain-based bonds.
Source: Own illustration

For investors, current challenges include the absence of these bonds on mainstream platforms, coupled with the need for new infrastructure and processes. Despite the obstacles, the tokenization aspect of blockchain-based bonds holds promise. Tokenization, which allows for investments in smaller denominations, could increase accessibility for retail investors. However, it is important to recognize that the implementation of blockchain technology itself does not change existing regulations, such as the Prospectus Regulation outlined in Section 2.1.2.1. As a result, retail investors' access to corporate bonds may remain limited. When corporations can place their volumes with institutional investors, too, they might not find it incentivizing enough to undertake the extra effort required to meet the stringent disclosure requirements for retail investors. This hypothesis could be tested in the context of other studies.

Blockchain-based bonds and traditional bonds have similar credit risks that depend on the issuer's creditworthiness. However, blockchain-based bonds face higher liquidity risks, primarily due to exchange-listing difficulties and ineligibility for ECB programs. Blockchain could reduce settlement risks with atomic settlements while current implementations rely on traditional banking for settlement in fiat currencies. As with any emerging technology, blockchain also brings increased technological risk, which is expected to decrease with further testing and integration. Yet, it remains to be seen whether and how this technological risk—which has already been recognized by rating agencies (Gusdorf, 2023)—might be reflected in bond ratings once more transactions have been conducted. Legal risks differ by jurisdiction. For instance, Germany—with its eWpG—has developed a more advanced legal framework for blockchain-based bonds. This framework aligns blockchain-based bonds' risk profiles closely to those of traditional bonds.

The results generally reflect the sentiment in the literature, for example Casey et al. (2018) or Axelsen et al. (2023), who assume significant risk improvement opportunities through blockchain if the challenges are overcome. Upon reaching notable milestones—for example in on-chain cash settlement—it would be worthwhile to revisit this analysis and verify if the expected results have materialized.

Cost-wise, traditional bonds incur considerable intermediary expenses throughout their lifecycle, which blockchain technology can potentially reduce by streamlining processes. However, the study concludes that the costs of issuing blockchain-based bonds are currently higher compared to traditional instruments. This difference is largely attributable to the need for foundational work and the absence of standardized processes, which affirms the observations of Saramago (2022). Conversely, Bauer et al. (2023) suggest that even in the existing setup, blockchain-based bonds entail significantly reduced costs compared to traditional bonds. However, they did not consider "all change costs incurred e.g., due to implementation efforts on the IT and business side" (p. 4). That limitation must be acknowledged when interpreting their results.

In the long-term perspective, nonetheless, the findings of this study support the perspective of Bauer et al. (2023). They predict that it will be possible to realize significant cost-saving potential when processing bonds on a blockchain relative to traditional channels. Similar perspectives on the cost benefits of leveraging blockchain for bond transactions have been expressed by scholars like Santo et al. (2016) or Pana and Gangal (2021).

Additionally, blockchain technology's role as a unified data source could extend its impact beyond the costs associated with issuing, trading, and custody. By eliminating the need for multiple systems and thus resolving data accuracy conflicts, efficiency could be significantly enhanced. This broader efficiency impact is also acknowledged in the work of Priem (2020). Yet, the status of realization and magnitude of these expected cost benefits remain key subjects for future academic investigation.

Moreover, blockchain technology enhances transparency in bond transactions by maintaining detailed histories of transactions between various wallets. If it becomes feasible for issuers to link real-world identities to wallet addresses, a more strategic interaction between issuers and investors could be fostered. However, how the disclosure of investor names to issuers could comply with data protection legislation is outside the scope of this study and should be discussed separately.

Without access to user identities, the utility of blockchain's transparency generally remains limited. Furthermore, the visibility of transaction histories to all network participants—even though anonymized—raises privacy concerns, particularly in public networks. Addressing these concerns requires the development of sophisticated privacy solutions within blockchain systems. These findings offer a more nuanced understanding of blockchain-enabled transparency, which is already well-documented in the literature, for example by Vakta et al. (2016) or Axelsen et al. (2023).

In summary, blockchain-based bonds currently exhibit challenges in accessibility due to a limited investor base and the necessity for new infrastructure but may offer long-term market-access benefits. They bear similar credit risks to traditional bonds but face distinct liquidity and technological risks. The currently higher costs of issuing blockchain-based bonds are attributed to initial investments and the lack of standardized processes, with potential long-term cost reductions through decreased intermediary expenses. Blockchain technology enhances transactional transparency but faces privacy concerns and limitations without user identity access. This analysis recognizes blockchain's current limitations while highlighting its potential to transform the bond market.

5.2 Benefits, Barriers, and Market-Adoption Dynamics

The second subordinate research question—"What are the perceived benefits of, and key barriers to, blockchain-based bonds, and what are current market-adoption dynamics?"—explores the advantages, challenges, and current trends in the adoption of blockchain-based bonds. This examination is crucial for understanding their practical implications. Assessing the primary barriers and benefits is key to predicting whether blockchain-based bonds will be widely adopted or encounter significant resistance, which directly influences their impact on the bond market.

Blockchain technology is broadly acknowledged for its potential to significantly transform the bond market, offering a range of benefits that could revolutionize the sector. It can drastically reduce settlement times from days to nearly instantaneous transactions, an aspect particularly crucial in large-scale institutional transactions where timing can significantly impact financial outcomes. Additionally, blockchain offers the possibility of integrating bond settlement and delivery into a single, immutable system, streamlining various back-office operations including risk management and accounting.

The integration of smart contracts into blockchain-based bonds processing represents a significant innovation in operational efficiency and compliance that could potentially enable automated and scalable funding processes. Blockchain's applicability extends to various financial instruments, suggesting its potential as a unifying technological standard in the financial sector. This integration could facilitate the seamless combination of different financial tools, which opens avenues for novel financial solutions.

The findings correspond with the research of scholars such as Vakta et al. (2016), Pinna and Ruttenberg (2016) and recently Bauer et al. (2023), who have recognized similar blockchain benefits in bond applications and in applications for securities in general. Nonetheless, the present study especially emphasizes the potential of blockchain to serve as a comprehensive technological standard for a variety of financial instruments beyond bonds, thereby enabling combinations to create innovative financial solutions. This perspective has not yet been thoroughly explored in the existing literature. It provides a new angle on blockchain's capabilities and its possible transformative impact on the financial industry.

Despite the potential of blockchain-based bonds, several barriers are hindering their widespread adoption. Many of these barriers are not unique to blockchain-based bonds but are common to blockchain implementations in various contexts. While experts contest some barriers noted in existing literature, they also identify new adoption challenges not previously covered. Table 5.2 presents a concise comparison of these barriers as discussed in literature and by experts, with a more detailed analysis provided in the subsequent section.

Experts have identified technological challenges, including fragmentation within the blockchain ecosystem and limited transaction throughput, as significant hurdles. This perspective aligns with the findings of researchers like Agbo et al. (2019) and Hafid et al. (2020), who have highlighted these issues as major barriers to blockchain implementation, as detailed in Section 2.2.9. In contrast, the expert opinions did not corroborate the role of high energy consumption, which is another potential barrier cited by Esmaeilian et al. (2020) and Weerawarna et al. (2023). The experts point to the energy efficiency of the PoS consensus mechanism, which significantly reduces energy consumption while maintaining a satisfactory level of security in comparison to PoW. Furthermore, unlike what is suggested in the literature, for instance by Porru et al. (2017), experts do not view underdevelopment of blockchain-related software as an implementation barrier.

From the perspective of the interviewed experts, organizational challenges encompass large investments required for infrastructure development, which are particularly burdensome for smaller firms, as well as complexities in managing

Table 5.2 Literature Versus Expert Opinions on Blockchain Implementation Barriers

Expert	Challenge	Literature	Interviews
Technological	Low transaction throughput	X	X
	Fragmentation / Lack of interoperability	X	X
	Insufficient software development	X	
	High energy consumption	X	
Organizational	Data privacy concerns	X	
	Unproven reliability	X	
	High resource deployment	X	X
	Shortfall in training / knowledge	X	X
	Problems in intra-company liquidity management due to instant settlement		X
Environmental	Lack of trust	X	
	Regulatory hurdles	X	X
	Lack of liquidity of blockchain-based bonds		X

Note: An "X" indicates that the challenge has been identified as a barrier for widespread adoption
Source: Own illustration

intra-company liquidity when transitioning to atomic settlements. While the former aligns well with the findings of Mishra et al. (2023), the latter introduces a new dimension to the existing body of literature. Its in-depth exploration and quantification could be a valuable pursuit for future research.

The study's experts identify the limited availability of skilled professionals, particularly of those with expertise in both IT and finance, as a concern in the adoption of blockchain-based bonds. Despite this, experts contend that the necessary skills can be developed internally, which suggests that the current talent shortage may not significantly impede the adoption of these bonds. However, a more critical concern noted is the lack of technological knowledge among management board members, who are instrumental in making strategic decisions on matters like the adoption of new technologies.

This observation is consistent with Pana and Gangal (2021), who point out that a lack of understanding of the technology is a major hurdle for the adoption of blockchain-based bonds. Similarly, Walsh et al. (2021) indicate that inadequate training or knowledge among employees, coupled with insufficient management support, can obstruct the effective implementation of blockchain technology. Conversely, while the unproven reliability of blockchain technology (Batubara et al., 2018) and data protection concerns (Weerawarna et al., 2023) are acknowledged as important considerations by the experts, they are generally not perceived as significant barriers to the scaling of blockchain-based bonds.

The analysis also highlights "environmental" factors as barriers to the implementation of blockchain-based bonds. While acknowledging the importance of trust in technology, the experts currently do not perceive a lack of trust as a significant issue, diverging from the observations of Yeoh (2017). Instead, they point to the limited liquidity of these bonds as a key obstacle, which is mainly driven by difficulties in enabling exchange listings and the lack of matured on-chain cash settlement options involving fiat currencies. These issues are seen as significant constraints on the growth of blockchain-based bonds. Furthermore, experts highlight the fragmented regulatory environment across different jurisdictions, emphasizing the need for harmonized legal frameworks to scale blockchain-based bonds.

While existing literature, including Priem (2020) as well as Pana and Gangal (2021), comprehensively acknowledges the regulatory hurdles as significant challenges to blockchain implementation, it barely touches upon issues like the liquidity challenges and the lack of matured on-chain cash settlement solutions involving fiat currencies. Expert interviews in this study, however, indicate that these factors are critical roadblocks to the scalability of blockchain-based bonds. Interviewees emphasize that, before widespread adoption of blockchain-based bonds can take place, these issues must be resolved.

The market adoption of blockchain-based bonds is still in an early, exploratory phase and is characterized by varying levels of engagement from different players. Transaction facilitators show keen interest, motivated by the potential benefits of blockchain and the fear of missing out on key technological advancements. In contrast, bond issuers are more reserved, adopting a "wait-and-see" approach and weighing technological progress against financial considerations. Investor demand, which significantly influences the adoption rate, is currently low, creating a "chicken and egg" situation where increased offerings of blockchain-based bonds could boost investor interest and vice versa. Experts consider it crucial to avoid eroding the general trust in technology, particularly through additional negative headlines, such as those related to the realm of cryptocurrencies.

Given the challenges outlined on both the issuer and investor sides, this early adoption status does not seem surprising. Consequently, the impact of blockchain-based bonds on corporate refinancing strategies remains limited at this stage. However, the potential benefits of blockchain in this area are clear, and market recognition appears to be growing. Hence, once the potential is realized to the extent that blockchain-based bonds are perceived as significantly better than traditional instruments, either by issuers or investors, it seems likely that these bonds will be established sustainably in the bond market.

A significant rise in blockchain-based bond issuances was observed in Germany in the past year. BaFin data indicates that 48 out of all 65 blockchain-based bond issues under eWpG—nearly 75%—occurred in 2023 (BaFin, 2023b). This surge suggests a potential acceleration in adoption in the coming years. However, it remains uncertain whether this trend signifies a long-term shift or is simply a short-term fluctuation. Currently, it is too early for a definitive prediction.

Yet, the specific impact of the DLT Pilot Regime on the market-adoption dynamics is considered limited. While it introduces capabilities for secondary markets and encourages collaboration between banks and regulators, its constraints—such as its volume limitations and temporary nature—are noted as barriers to substantial engagement. However, experts suggest that leveraging this regime for gaining practical experience is vital for influencing future regulatory changes. This approach is seen as crucial for advancing broader implementation of digital securities. These observations provide a direct response to Zaccaroni (2022), who left the question of the industry's response to the DLT Pilot Regime open in his paper. In light of these findings, continuously observing and analyzing the Regime's evolution to grasp emerging trends and insights is imperative.

In summary, blockchain-based bonds offer transformative potential in the bond market but currently face significant challenges to widespread adoption. These include technological issues, like ecosystem fragmentation; organizational barriers, such as the high cost of setting up necessary infrastructure; and "environmental" factors, like limited liquidity and diverse regulatory frameworks. Overcoming these challenges is crucial for fully leveraging blockchain's potential in this sector. Transaction facilitators are actively exploring blockchain-based bonds, while issuers approach them with caution. Investor demand is slowly emerging, largely influenced by trust in the technology. A recent rise in blockchain-based bond issuances in Germany indicates growing market interest. Given its restrictions, the impact of the DLT Pilot Regime on market dynamics, however, remains limited. Nonetheless, it should be used to gain practical insights and to help to shape future regulation.

5.3 Transformation of Intermediary and Infrastructure-Provider Roles

The third subordinate research question—"How can blockchain technology transform the roles and functions of market intermediaries and infrastructure providers in the context of bond markets?"—examines the potential impact of widespread blockchain adoption on these entities. Blockchain's distinctive features could simplify traditional roles or even render some of them obsolete. These changes could possibly lead to a significant transformation of the functions of market intermediaries and infrastructure providers.

It is important to note that, in Germany, only the roles of the registrar and the CSD for exchange listings are currently mandated by law. However, the present paper concludes that extensive disintermediation in the market is unlikely. Instead, it anticipates an evolution of traditional intermediary roles, accompanied by the emergence of new roles, with both sets of roles providing diverse services throughout a bond's lifecycle. However, these roles do not necessarily have to be filled by traditional intermediaries. They could also be assumed by other entities—particularly smaller, more specialized companies—which would likely intensify competition in the sector.

Investment banks, traditionally central to bond issuance, might adapt to potential changes brought about by blockchain technology. Their role in ensuring compliance, particularly in managing complex regulatory processes like KYC, will likely remain crucial. Yet, their involvement in market access and bond placement will likely become more nuanced. While blockchain enables direct issuer-investor interactions, potentially reducing banks' roles in these areas, their importance in market access will largely depend on the issuer's market recognition and experience with bond issuances. Well-established, more experienced issuers might find it easier to engage with investors directly. Conversely, smaller, or less experienced companies may still rely heavily on investment banks for these services.

Clearinghouses and CSDs face the possibility of either redundancy or significant role evolution due to blockchain's capacity to automate many of their traditional functions. They may adapt to roles like those of coordinators or rulesetters. The necessity for CSDs to fundamentally alter their business model hinges on regulatory opening toward putting decentralized financial products on an equal footing with traditional ones. Custodian banks might transition toward the role of crypto custodians and safeguard digital assets. Despite the self-custody capabilities afforded by blockchain, the expertise and support of custodian banks presumably will remain in demand, particularly by private investors. These observations are line with Bauer et al. (2023), who also attribute the greatest potential for blockchain-enabled cost savings in the area of clearing, settlement and asset servicing, with the latter including coupon payments and redemption.

Integrating blockchain technology introduces new roles like crypto registrars and platform providers. Highlighted by the eWpG, crypto registrars are essential for maintaining accurate token records and ensuring compliance with legal standards. Simultaneously, platform providers are key in developing and managing infrastructure, which is crucial for secondary-market trading of digital assets.

This overall assessment significantly challenges the concept of complete disintermediation, as proposed by Vakta et al. (2016). Even if it would be legally feasible, complete elimination of intermediary services would not necessarily be practical, which is a viewpoint shared by Lee (2018). Automation can handle certain steps in the bond lifecycle, but—in the case of complete disintermediation—other aspects would require direct involvement from issuers or investors. The consideration that self-management may not consistently be perceived as advantageous by all parties indicates that there will be an ongoing need for intermediaries. These intermediaries, continually striving to adapt to new market conditions, might offer issuers and investors the flexibility to select and tailor additional services to meet their specific needs. As the market evolves, it will become clearer which intermediary services are deemed crucial and which might become obsolete.

5.4 Outlook

Finally, the answer to the fourth subordinate research question—"How do experts assess the future development of blockchain-based bonds?"—synthesizes expert opinions on the trajectory of blockchain-based bonds. These expert insights are key for anticipating emerging trends and understanding the potential effects of blockchain-based bonds on corporate financing and the bond market.

Experts offer diverse opinions on the future of blockchain-based bonds, stressing the importance of setting industry standards for efficiency and interoperability. A central debate revolves around the choice between private and public networks. Some experts lean toward private networks due to their control, governance, and compliance to regulatory frameworks that is relatively simple to ensure, while others favor public blockchains for their scalability and wider market access despite higher transaction costs. In public networks, the consensus-mechanism choice is a unanimous point among experts. They point to PoS because it offers energy efficiency compared to PoW, while simultaneously maintaining a robust level of security. This point implicitly touches upon the call for research of Collomb and Sok (2016) to identify a suitable consensus mechanism.

The future path of blockchain-based bonds, whether toward private or public networks, is yet to be determined. It will likely be influenced by evolving technological capabilities, regulatory developments—especially the implementation of recommendations from the BCBS—and overall market dynamics. This situation parallels the observations of Choudhury et al. (2023), who outline comparable advantages and disadvantages of the different network types, lending support to these conclusions. Yet, while advocating for standards, they similarly stop short of endorsing a specific network type as a recommendation for blockchain-based bonds.

In addition, the importance of blockchain-based bonds in the digitalization of the bond market is discussed. Experts hold varied opinions on the role blockchain-based bonds will play. Some anticipate that blockchain-based bonds could replace traditional bonds, whereas others view them as complementary, especially in sectors like ESG. Meanwhile, some experts express skepticism about blockchain as the leading technology for digitalizing bond issuance, citing centralized alternatives like D7, which maintain the appearance and market depth of traditional bonds. However, opting for centralized solutions, in turn, would come at the expense of advantages offered by decentralized solutions, such as P2P trading or immutability.

According to expert opinions, the prevailing solution will be the one offering the most advantageous cost-benefit ratio. The potential advantages of blockchain are substantial, yet they come with the need for extensive changes throughout the bond market infrastructure, down to the level of intra-organizational processes. Considering the extent of these required transformations, the expert consensus appears rational: If blockchain-based solutions are to succeed, their widespread adoption in corporate financing will likely be the result of a gradual, long-lasting process rather than an immediate overhaul.

This assessment is consistent with the prediction of Mori (2016) that the full integration of blockchain technology into financial infrastructure will span several years. Yet, given the current pace of development, their upper-bound estimate of a decade appears overly optimistic. To date, there has been relatively little progress in terms of actual implementation. Therefore, it is not surprising that the development prospects that experts currently see remain largely generic and unchanged from those already described some years ago by Collomb and Sok (2016) as well as by Pinna and Ruttenberg (2016). Nonetheless, the results confirm the observations of Pana and Gangal (2021) that recent advancements, such as those made by regulators, are expediting the adoption of blockchain-based bond issuances.

In conclusion, there is a significant debate among experts about the future of blockchain-based bonds. This debate centers on choosing between private and public networks, which is a question influenced by technological advancements, regulatory frameworks, and overall market trends. Experts present mixed views on the importance of the role of blockchain-based bonds in the digitalization of the bond market: Some foresee blockchain-based bonds replacing traditional bonds, while others view them as a complementary solution for certain fields. The discussion also considers alternative approaches to bond market digitization, such as centralized solutions like D7. However, these approaches could not exploit the advantages that decentralized solutions offer, such as P2P trading or immutability.

Experts generally concur that the technology offering the most advantageous overall cost-benefit ratio will likely dominate the market and corporate financing in the long-term. However, should blockchain-based solutions prevail in the end, it is expected that the path of adoption will have been gradual and protracted.

Conclusion 6

6.1 Summary of Findings

In conclusion, this research provides a comprehensive analysis on the impact of blockchain-based bonds on corporate financing and the bond-market setup, focusing on Germany. Insights from 19 experts—analyzed using a qualitative approach that combines different methodologies defined by Mayring (2015)—reveal several key findings. The findings are succinctly visualized in Fig. 6.1 and presented in more detail in the following section.

In the long-term, blockchain-based bonds may offer distinct advantages with regard to accessibility, overall risk, cost, and transparency compared to traditional bonds. However, these advantages are not fully realizable in the current setup. Blockchain-based bonds promise easier access to capital markets and lower issuance costs but currently face higher liquidity risks due to challenges with traditional exchange listings and non-eligibility for ECB programs. Technologically, the novelty of blockchain introduces elevated risks, which are expected to decrease over time. While varying between jurisdictions, legal risks in Germany are closely aligned with traditional bonds due to the eWpG. Cost benefits from streamlined processes are currently outweighed by the high costs of setting up the necessary infrastructure. Yet, long-term advantages include cheaper issuances that allow for continuous refinancing, and hence better risk management. Transparency is enhanced, offering detailed transaction histories, but the full benefits of this transparency can only be realized if issuers have access to real investor identities.

Market adoption of blockchain-based bonds is currently at an early stage, with transaction facilitators showing eagerness due to potential benefits and to the fear

M. M. Grossmann, *Blockchain-Based Bonds*, BestMasters,
https://doi.org/10.1007/978-3-658-45311-4_6

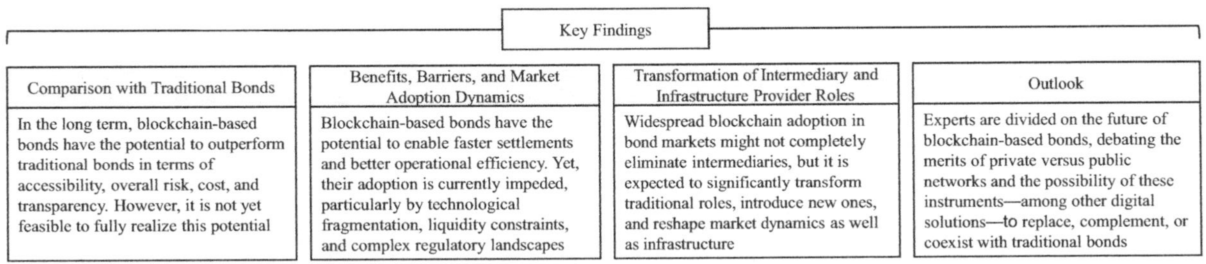

Fig. 6.1 Key Findings of the Study. (Source: Own illustration)

of missing out on advancements. Bond issuers remain reserved, balancing technological progress with financial implications. Key barriers to adoption include technological fragmentation, organizational challenges in intra-company liquidity management, large investments required for infrastructure, and environmental factors like limited liquidity and regulatory fragmentation. The DLT Pilot Regime, while beneficial for secondary-market capabilities and regulatory collaboration, is limited by volume restrictions and its temporary nature. Thus, its impact on market-adoption dynamics remains limited.

Widespread adoption of blockchain-based bonds may transform the roles of market intermediaries and infrastructure providers. Investment banks may retain vital roles in compliance and market access, especially for less experienced issuers. Other entities, like clearinghouses and CSDs, may become obsolete or evolve, while custodian banks might transition to crypto custodians. Emerging roles, such as crypto registrars and platform providers, are integral to the blockchain-based bond ecosystem.

Experts are debating both the most suitable network type for convergence and, generally, the future of blockchain-based bonds. Private networks offer control, governance, and relatively simple alignment with regulatory frameworks, while public networks provide scalability and wider market access. According to the experts, the future could see blockchain-based bonds replacing traditional ones, serving as complementary solutions in areas like ESG funding, or being surpassed by alternative, centralized digital methods like D7. This variety of possible outcomes emphasizes the need for a deep understanding of both technology and financial markets.

Overall, blockchain-based bonds have significant potential to transform corporate financing as well as the bond market, and hence to be a real "game changer" in the world of corporate financing. However, their full adoption and impact hinge on addressing various challenges, regulatory evolution, and overall market dynamics, which makes it a promising field for continued research and exploration.

6.2 Future Research Directions

Exploring blockchain-based bonds in corporate financing and bond markets opens avenues for crucial future research, which would advance the understanding of blockchain technology's integration and long-term impact in financial systems. Some of these opportunities have already been highlighted in the course of this study; some more general ones will be outlined in this chapter.

One vital area for future investigation is the real-world application and enduring impact of blockchain-based bonds, particularly once matured on-chain cash settlement solutions around fiat currencies have been integrated. Longitudinal studies tracking the market performance and acceptance of these bonds over time would be essential to assess their sustainability and efficacy in corporate finance.

Moreover, in-depth comparative case studies between blockchain-based and traditional bond issuances, considering varied market environments and regulatory frameworks, would be key to identifying conditions that favor the effectiveness of blockchain-based bonds.

Further investigating the transformation of roles among traditional financial intermediaries and infrastructure providers in the wake of blockchain adoption presents another promising research path. Detailed case studies of institutions adapting to this technological shift could offer valuable lessons and insights. Thoroughly examining how these entities redefine their roles and services in response to blockchain adoption could provide practical guidance for other market participants undergoing similar transformations.

Additionally, a comparative analysis with blockchain alternatives for improving processes across the bond's lifecycle—like centralized solutions such as D7—would be crucial to elucidate the competitive dynamics and factors driving technology choices in bond markets. Assessing efficiencies, costs, and market responses to different technological solutions will help to identify the most viable and promising methods for future bond issuances.

In summary, these proposed research directions focus on practical, regulatory, and comparative aspects of blockchain technology in bond markets, offering a comprehensive framework for future exploration. They aim to deepen the collective understanding of the transformative impact of blockchain technology on corporate financing and bond markets, highlighting both opportunities and challenges.

6.3 Implications

The following section presents the theoretical and practical implications of the results of this research in detail.

6.3.1 Theoretical Implications

This research on blockchain-based bonds builds upon the foundational works of scholars such as Pinna and Ruttenberg (2016) and Petrov (2019). While these studies have provided a broad overview of DLT's potential in financial institutions, the present paper narrows the focus to specifically examine blockchain's role in bond markets, particularly in terms of accessibility, risk, cost, and transparency. This approach not only delves deeper into the specific applications of blockchain in bond issuance and lifecycle management in a German context, but also offers a more nuanced understanding of the opportunities and challenges presented by this technology.

The present study addresses scalability and interoperability issues highlighted by Collomb and Sok (2016) and Casey et al. (2018) and explores how these challenges materialize in the bond-market context. It acknowledges the complexities identified in previous research and investigates the practical integration of blockchain into financial markets, providing a clearer picture of its real-world application. By focusing on expert opinions, this study offers a grounded perspective on the regulatory challenges and opportunities in blockchain-based bonds, complementing the broader regulatory discussions presented by Casey et al. (2018) and Lehmann (2021).

Building upon the insights of Mortensen (2021), who highlighted DLT's burgeoning influence on post-trade processes, this research expands the discussion by offering empirical insights into the actual implementation challenges and benefits in bond markets from the perspective of bond issuers, transaction facilitators and the capital market's buy-side. It complements the work of Mori (2016), who discussed the barriers to blockchain integration, and Popescu (2020), who assessed how digital assets transform capital markets, with a specific focus on corporate bonds.

Furthermore, the present study extends beyond the theoretical models and advocacy for blockchain in securities as presented by Vakta et al. (2016) or Bauvars and Kirikova (2021). It goes a step further by offering practical insights into the actual implementation in the bond markets and by elaborating on perceived challenges and benefits, thus adding depth to the existing body of literature. Complementing the work of Pana and Gangal (2021) and Saramago (2022), who highlighted the potential and limitations of blockchain in bonds, this research adds another dimension—a practical perspective—to their findings by leveraging expert interviews. Moreover, it adds a qualitative perspective to the quantitative analysis of Bauer et al. (2023), who emphasized the significant cost-saving potential of DLT within capital market infrastructures.

Most existing studies in this field are predominantly theoretical. This research aims to bridge this gap by incorporating practical insights from industry experts, thus providing a more grounded understanding of blockchain's impact on bond markets. The findings from these expert interviews offer a basis for future research to explore the evolving landscape of blockchain in bond markets, potentially guiding future implementation as well as policy making and regulatory developments. In summary, this research extends the existing body of literature by enriching the theoretical discourse with real-world perspectives and offers a comprehensive insight into the present evolution of blockchain-based bonds.

6.3.2 Practical Implications

The emergence of blockchain-based bonds in corporate financing introduces significant practical implications for market stakeholders, particularly in light of the research findings. This chapter outlines these implications, drawing direct connections to the research results.

Blockchain-based bonds could provide an innovative and accessible capital-raising method that is particularly beneficial for SMEs. They may democratize access to the bond market, which is currently constrained by traditional structures. Also, large corporations should consider blockchain-based bonds due to their potential in dynamic risk management and continuous market access, as highlighted in the findings.

The tokenization aspect of blockchain-based bonds may offer smaller denominations and increased accessibility, especially for retail investors. Yet, this development also depends on the decisions of the issuers as to whether they will make their bonds accessible to such investors, as this approach could entail additional expenses. However, the currently higher liquidity risks, stemming from limited exchange listings and secondary-market constraints, would need to be factored into investment strategies. This aspect is crucial for informed investment decisions given the distinct liquidity and market dynamics of blockchain-based bonds compared to traditional bonds.

The evolving regulatory landscape, especially in jurisdictions like Germany, is becoming more conducive to blockchain-based bonds. However, in regions with less regulatory clarity, these bonds may face higher legal risks. Companies and investors would need to strategically navigate this uneven regulatory environment, with a focus on compliance, especially in complex processes like KYC.

In the blockchain era, traditional market intermediaries, including investment banks, clearinghouses, CSDs, and custodian banks, may need to adapt to—partly significant—changes in their roles to maintain relevance. As blockchain technology could reshape the financial landscape, many of the tasks traditionally performed by these institutions may become obsolete or require transformation. Furthermore, the emergence of smaller, specialized companies poised to enter the market might introduce increased competition. This evolving scenario emphasizes the critical need for established financial institutions to demonstrate agility and innovation. Embracing new roles and adapting to the unique demands of blockchain-based bond transactions might be essential for their continued success and relevance in this rapidly changing environment.

Addressing technological barriers such as fragmentation and interoperability is essential for the broader adoption of blockchain-based bonds. This assessment aligns with the research findings that emphasize the need for large investments in infrastructure and the reaching of agreement on standards. Hence, a collaborative approach among market participants is vital to fully realize the benefits of blockchain in bond markets.

The research suggests a complex and evolving role for blockchain in bond markets. In the short term, blockchain-based bonds are identified as complementary solutions, particularly in specialized areas like ESG financing. A significant shift toward blockchain-based bonds, although possible in the long term, is expected to be rather gradual. The exploration of alternative, centralized digitization methods, such as D7, indicates a market openness to diverse technological approaches. Hence, it is important for stakeholders to stay informed and adaptable to the evolving market dynamics, balancing traditional practices with innovative digital solutions in corporate financing.

In summary, this research underscores the significant practical implications of blockchain-based bonds in corporate financing. They may present new capital-raising avenues, introduce changes in accessibility and risk profiles, and necessitate adaptations in regulatory compliance and intermediary roles. Stakeholders must navigate these evolving dynamics with strategic flexibility, integrating innovative digital solutions with established financial practices.

6.4 Limitations

This research, while providing valuable insights into blockchain-based bonds, is subject to certain limitations that must be acknowledged.

Firstly, the study relies on Germany as a case study. While offering in-depth local insights, the generalizability of the findings may be limited. Variations in regulatory environments, market dynamics, and technological adoption rates across different countries could influence the broader applicability of the results.

Secondly, the reliance on expert interviews, although providing nuanced perspectives, inherently introduces subjectivity to the study. The views and experiences of these experts, while valuable, are individual and may not accurately represent the broader market consensus. Additionally, the engagement with the capital market's buy-side was notably limited, represented by a single interview. This limitation resulted in an underrepresentation of this stakeholder group, which potentially could have led to skewed insights.

The focus on senior professionals from banking, fintech, industrial corporations, and asset management provided in-depth insights but might have led to a homogeneity of perspectives. The inclusion of a more diverse range of stakeholders, for instance regulatory authorities and FMIs, would likely have offered a broader spectrum of viewpoints. This approach could have provided a more nuanced understanding of the complexities and implications associated with blockchain-based bonds.

Thirdly, it is important to note that some interviews were conducted in English, which was not the first language of either the interviewer or the interviewee. This might have led to a potential loss of linguistic subtleties, potentially affecting the interpretation of the data collected.

Fourthly, the qualitative nature of the research limits the potential to quantify findings or draw statistical generalizations. While qualitative insights are crucial for understanding complex phenomena like blockchain adoption in bond markets, they do not offer the empirical robustness that quantitative data might offer. This limitation becomes particularly significant when assessing growth trajectories and the economic impact of blockchain-based bonds. In such cases, quantitative data, once it becomes broadly available, could yield complementary conclusions.

Fifthly, the absence of an inter-coder reliability check, and the reliance on a single method of triangulation present a notable limitation in the applied methodology. Inter-coder reliability checks are commonly used in qualitative research to ensure consistency in qualitative data interpretation, as they involve multiple researchers independently coding the data. However, given the lack of a research peer, this tool could not be applied to the present study. This shortcoming, in turn, may have affected the objectivity of the findings.

Additionally, triangulation, encompassing multiple methods or data sources for validation, was limited to a single approach. While data-source triangulation was effectively implemented, other forms, like investigator triangulation—which involves engaging multiple researchers to cross-check research findings—were not conducted. As a result, the findings should be interpreted with an understanding that broader triangulation could have had enhanced their robustness and validity. Despite incorporating other stringent quality measures such as communicative validation, it is possible that these methodological limitations may not have been completely mitigated. These limitations should be considered when evaluating the study's reliability and credibility.

Lastly, the rapidly evolving nature of blockchain technology and its applications in financial markets could result in the findings of this study having a limited "shelf life." Technological advancements, regulatory changes, and shifts in market adoption could quickly alter the landscape. These developments could make the insights and conclusions drawn in this study less relevant or outdated in a short period.

In conclusion, this research provides important insights into the potential and challenges of blockchain-based bonds in corporate financing. However, it is crucial to consider the outlined limitations, particularly regarding the geographical focus of the study, its methodological approach, and the evolving nature of blockchain technology, when interpreting the findings and applying them to broader contexts.

References

Abou Jaoude, J., & Saade, R. G. (2019). Blockchain applications—Usage in different domains. *IEEE Access, 7.*

Abrol, A. (2023). *How many Bitcoins are there and how many are left to mine?* Blockchain Council. Retrieved January 12, 2024, from https://www.blockchain-council.org/cryptocurrency/how-many-bitcoins-are-left/

Adhami, S., Giudici, G., & Martinazzi, S. (2018). Why do businesses go crypto? An empirical analysis of initial coin offerings. *Journal of Economics and Business, 100*, 64–75.

Agbo, C. C., Mahmoud, Q. H., & Eklund, J. M. (2019). Blockchain technology in healthcare: A systematic review. *Healthcare, 7*(2), 56.

Aggarwal, S., & Kumar, N. (2021). Attacks on blockchain. In *Advances in Computers* (Vol. 121, pp. 399–410). Elsevier.

Alam, S., Shuaib, M., Khan, W. Z., Garg, S., Kaddoum, G., Hossain, M. S., & Zikria, Y. B. (2021). Blockchain-based initiatives: Current state and challenges. *Computer Networks, 198.*

AlShamsi, M., Al-Emran, M., & Shaalan, K. (2022). A Systematic Review on Blockchain Adoption. *Applied Sciences, 12*(9).

Alt, R., Beck, R., & Smits, M. T. (2018). Fintech and the transformation of the financial industry. *Electronic Markets, 28*(3), 235–243.

Altman, E., Resti, A., & Sironi, A. (2004). Default recovery rates in credit risk modelling: A review of the literature and empirical evidence. *Economic Notes, 33*(2), 183–208.

Amato, J. D., & Remolona, E. M. (2003). The credit spread puzzle. *BIS Quarterly Review, December.*

Angelis, J., & Da Silva, E. R. (2019). Blockchain adoption: A value driver perspective. *Business Horizons, 62*(3), 307–314.

Axelsen, H., Rasmussen, U., Jensen, J. R., Ross, O., & Henglein, F. (2023). Trading green bonds using distributed ledger technology. *ECIS 2023 Research Papers.*

BaFin (2023a, November 15). *Bond prospectus regime.* Bundesanstalt fuer Finanzdienstleistungsaufsicht. Retrieved January 12, 2024, from https://www.bafin.de/EN/Aufsicht/Prospekte/Wertpapiere/Basisprospektregime/basisprospektregime_artikel_en.html

BaFin (2023b, January 3, 2024). *Kryptowertpapierliste nach eWpG.* Bundesanstalt fuer Finanzdienstleistungsaufsicht. Retrieved January 12, 2024, from https://www.bafin.de/DE/PublikationenDaten/Datenbanken/Kryptowertpapiere/kryptowerte_node.html

M. M. Grossmann, *Blockchain-Based Bonds*, BestMasters,
https://doi.org/10.1007/978-3-658-45311-4

Baker, M., & Wurgler, J. (2002). Market timing and capital structure. *The Journal of Finance, 57*(1), 1–32.

Bao, J., Pan, J., & Wang, J. (2011). The illiquidity of corporate bonds. *The Journal of Finance, 66*(3), 911–946.

Batubara, F. R., Ubacht, J., & Janssen, M. (2018). Challenges of blockchain technology adoption for e-government: A systematic literature review. Proceedings of the 19th Annual International Conference on Digital Government Research: Governance in the Data Age.

Batwa, A., & Norrman, A. (2020). A framework for exploring blockchain technology in supply chain management. *Operations and Supply Chain Management: An International Journal, 13*(3), 294–306.

Baucas, M. J., Spachos, P., & Plataniotis, K. N. (2021). Public-key reinforced blockchain platform for fog-IoT network system administration. *IEEE Internet of Things Journal, 9*(22).

Bauer, M., Sturz, D., Scheungraber, B., Liebscher, S., Censkowsky, S., & Ludwig, M. (2023). *Cost savings potential of DLT based capital market infrastructure—A quantitative analysis.*

Bauvars, J., & Kirikova, M. (2021). Blockchain applicability for securities settlement. BIR Workshops.

BCBS (2018). *Basel Committee Charter.* Basel Committee on Banking Supervision.

BCBS (2022). *Prudential treatment of cryptoasset exposures.* Basel Committee on Banking Supervision.

BCBS (2023). *Cryptoasset standard amendments.* Basel Committee on Banking Supervision

Becker, J., Breuker, D., Heide, T., Holler, J., Rauer, H. P., & Boehme, R. (2013). Can we afford integrity by proof-of-work? Scenarios inspired by the Bitcoin currency. *Workshop on the Economics of Information Security WEIS 2012.*

Bessembinder, H., & Maxwell, W. (2008). Markets: Transparency and the corporate bond market. *Journal of Economic Perspectives, 22*(2), 217–234.

Bhandarkar, V. V., Bhandarkar, A. A., & Shiva, A. (2019). Digital stocks using blockchain technology the possible future of stocks? *International Journal of Management, 10*(3).

BIS (2023). *Summary of debt securities outstanding.*

Bloomberg (2024). *German stock index DAX.* Bloomberg Terminal.

Bogner, A., Littig, B., & Menz, W. (2009). *Interviewing experts.* Springer.

Bogner, A., Littig, B., & Menz, W. (2014). *Interviews mit Experten: Eine praxisorientierte Einfuehrung* [Interviews with experts: A practice-oriented introduction]. Springer.

Bonneau, J., Miller, A., Clark, J., Narayanan, A., Kroll, J. A., & Felten, E. W. (2015). SoK: Research perspectives and challenges for Bitcoin and cryptocurrencies. 2015 IEEE Symposium on Security and Privacy,

Bord, V., & Santos, J. A. (2012). The rise of the originate-to-distribute model and the role of banks in financial intermediation. *Economic Policy Review, 18*(2), 21–34.

Bruehl, V. (2017). Bitcoins, Blockchain, and Distributed Ledgers: Funktionsweise, Marktentwicklungen und Zukunftsperspektiven [Bitcoins, blockchain, and distributed ledgers: functionality, market developments and future prospects]. *Wirtschaftsdienst, 97*, 135–142.

Burgess, K., & Colangelo, J. (2015). The promise of Bitcoin and the blockchain. *Consumers' Research.*

Buterin, V. (2014). A next-generation smart contract and decentralized application platform. *3*(37), 2–1.
Buterin, V., & Griffith, V. (2017). Casper the friendly finality gadget. *ArXiv*.
Buterin, V., Hernandez, D., Kamphefner, T., Pham, K., Qiao, Z., Ryan, D., Sin, J., Wang, Y., & Zhang, Y. X. (2020). Combining GHOST and Casper. *ArXiv*.
Cai, N., Helwege, J., & Warga, A. (2007). Underpricing in the corporate bond market. *The Review of Financial Studies*, *20*(6), 2021–2046.
Casey, M., Crane, J., Gensler, G., Johnson, S., & Narula, N. (2018). The impact of blockchain technology on finance: A catalyst for change. *Geneva Reports on the World Economy*.
Cashlink (2021). *Kryptowertpapiere und Security Tokens im direkten Vergleich* [Crypto securities and security tokens in direct comparison].
Celik, S., Demirtas, G., & Isaksson, M. (2015). Corporate bonds, bondholders and corporate governance.
Chang, A., El-Rayes, N., & Shi, J. (2022). Blockchain technology for supply chain management: A comprehensive review. *FinTech*, *1*(2), 191–205.
Chen, J. (2022). An overview of bond pricing models and duration of bonds. 2022 7th International Conference on Financial Innovation and Economic Development (ICFIED 2022),
Choudhury, R., Jhanji, K., Samd, H., Gleeson, S., & Bennett, S. (2023). Impact of distributed ledger technology in global capital markets.
Christensen, J. (2008). The corporate bond credit spread puzzle. *FRBSF Economic Letter*.
Christidis, K., & Devetsikiotis, M. (2016). Blockchains and smart contracts for the internet of things. *IEEE Access*, *4*, 2292–2303.
Christodoulou, P., Psillaki, M., Sklias, G., & Chatzichristofis, S. A. (2023). A blockchain-based framework for effective monitoring of EU green bonds. *Finance Research Letters*, *58*.
Clearstream (2019). *Clearstream snapshot*.
Clohessy, T., & Acton, T. (2019). Investigating the influence of organizational factors on blockchain adoption: An innovation theory perspective. *Industrial Management & Data Systems*, *119*(7), 1457–1491.
Cocco, L., & Marchesi, M. (2016). Modeling and simulation of the economics of mining in the Bitcoin market. *PloS One*, *11*(10).
Cocco, L., Pinna, A., & Marchesi, M. (2017). Banking on blockchain: Costs savings thanks to the blockchain technology. *Future Internet*, *9*(3), 25.
Cohen, G. (2022). Algorithmic trading and financial forecasting using advanced artificial intelligence methodologies. *Mathematics*, *10*(18), 3302.
Collomb, A., & Sok, K. (2016). Blockchain/distributed ledger technology (DLT): What impact on the financial sector? *Digiworld Economic Journal*(103).
Cortes-Goicoechea, M., Mohandas-Daryanani, T., Munoz-Tapia, J. L., & Bautista-Gomez, L. (2023). Autopsy of Ethereum's post-merge reward system. *ArXiv*.
Croman, K., Decker, C., Eyal, I., Gencer, A. E., Juels, A., Kosba, A., Miller, A., Saxena, P., Shi, E., & Guen Sirer, E. (2016). On scaling decentralized blockchains: A position paper. International Conference on Financial Cryptography and Data Security.
Crosby, M., Pattanayak, P., Verma, S., & Kalyanaraman, V. (2016). Blockchain technology: Beyond Bitcoin. *Applied Innovation*, *2*(6–10), 71.

Dai, H.-N., Zheng, Z., & Zhang, Y. (2019). Blockchain for internet of things: A survey. *IEEE Internet of Things Journal*, *6*(5), 8076–8094.

De Jong, F., & Driessen, J. (2006). Liquidity risk premia in corporate bond markets. *The Quarterly Journal of Finance*.

Dinh, T. T. A., Wang, J., Chen, G., Liu, R., Ooi, B. C., & Tan, K.-L. (2017). Blockbench: A framework for analyzing private blockchains. Proceedings of the 2017 ACM International Conference on Management of Data.

Dominguez Anguiano, T., & Parte, L. (2023). The state of art, opportunities and challenges of blockchain in the insurance industry: A systematic literature review. *Management Review Quarterly*, 1–22.

Dresing, T., & Pehl, T. (2015). *Praxisbuch Interview, Transkription & Analyse. Anleitungen und Regelsysteme fuer qualitativ Forschende* [Practice book interview, transcription & analysis. Instructions and rule systems for qualitative researchers] (8 ed.). Dr Dresing & Pehl GmbH.

Durbin, E., & Ng, D. (2005). The sovereign ceiling and emerging market corporate bond spreads. *Journal of International Money and Finance*, *24*(4), 631–649.

Efanov, D., & Roschin, P. (2018). The all-pervasiveness of the blockchain technology. *Procedia Computer Science*, *123*, 116–121.

ESMA (2022). *Report on the DLT Pilot Regime*.

Esmaeilian, B., Sarkis, J., Lewis, K., & Behdad, S. (2020). Blockchain for the future of sustainable supply chain management in industry 4.0. *Resources, Conservation and Recycling*, *163*.

Esmat, A., de Vos, M., Ghiassi-Farrokhfal, Y., Palensky, P., & Epema, D. (2021). A novel decentralized platform for peer-to-peer energy trading market with blockchain technology. *Applied Energy*, *282*.

Ethereum (2023a, May 31). *ERC-20 token standard*. Retrieved January 12, 2024, from https://www.ethereum.org/en/developers/docs/standards/tokens/erc-20/

Ethereum (2023b, May 31). *The merge*. Retrieved January 12, 2024, from https://www.ethereum.org/en/roadmap/merge/

Ethereum (2023c, September 26). *Proof-of-stake*. Retrieved January 12, 2024, from https://www.ethereum.org/en/developers/docs/consensus-mechanisms/pos/

Ethereum (2023d, July 18). *Proof-of-stake rewards and penalties*. Retrieved January 12, 2024, from https://www.ethereum.org/en/developers/docs/consensus-mechanisms/pos/rewards-and-penalties/

Ethereum (2023e, July 26). *Proof-of-stake vs. proof-of-work*. Retrieved January 12, 2024, from https://www.ethereum.org/en/developers/docs/consensus-mechanisms/pos/pos-vs-pow/

Ethereum (2023f, December 15). *Roadmap*. Retrieved January 12, 2024, from https://www.ethereum.org/en/roadmap

EU (2014a). *Directive on markets in financial instruments*.

EU (2014b). *Regulation on improving securities settlement in the European Union and on central securities depositories*.

EU (2014c). *Regulation on markets in financial instruments*.

EU (2017). *Regulation on the prospectus to be published when securities are offered to the public or admitted to trading on a regulated market*.

EU (2022). *Regulation on a pilot regime for market infrastructures based on distributed ledger technology.*
EU (2023). *Regulation on markets in crypto-assets.*
eWpG (2021). *Gesetz ueber Elektronische Wertpapiere* [Electronic Securities Act]. Bundesgesetzblatt Teil I
eWpRV (2022). *Verordnung ueber Anforderungen an Elektronische Wertpapierregister* [Requirements for Electronic Securities Registers]. Bundesgesetzblatt Teil I
Fairfield, J. (2022). Tokenized: The law of non-fungible tokens and unique digital property. *Indiana Law Journal, 97*, 1261–1313.
Freshfields (2023). *DLT Pilot Regime—A navigator.*
Gabbi, G., & Sironi, A. (2005). Which factors affect corporate bonds pricing? Empirical evidence from eurobonds primary market spreads. *The European Journal of Finance, 11*(1), 59–74.
Gangwal, A., Gangavalli, H. R., & Thirupathi, A. (2023). A survey of layer-two blockchain protocols. *Journal of Network and Computer Applications, 209.*
Garay, U., Gonzalez, M., & Rosso, J. (2019). Country and industry effects in corporate bond spreads in emerging markets. *Journal of Business Research, 102*, 191–200.
Gaur, N. (2020). Blockchain challenges in adoption. *Managerial Finance, 46*(6), 849–858.
Gazi, P., Kiayias, A., & Russell, A. (2018). Stake-bleeding attacks on proof-of-stake blockchains. 2018 Crypto Valley Conference on Blockchain Technology (CVCBT).
Gebraselase, B. G., Helvik, B. E., & Jiang, Y. (2021). Effect of miner incentive on the confirmation time of Bitcoin transactions. 2021 IEEE International Conference on Blockchain.
Goldberg, J., & Nozawa, Y. (2021). Liquidity supply in the corporate bond market. *The Journal of Finance, 76*(2), 755–796.
Guedes, S. S., & Pinto, J. M. (2023). Pricing of project finance bonds: A comparative analysis of primary market spreads. *Journal of Corporate Finance*, 102429.
Guegan, D. (2017). Public blockchain versus private blockhain.
Guest, G., Bunce, A., & Johnson, L. (2006). How many interviews are enough? An experiment with data saturation and variability. *Field Methods, 18*(1), 59–82.
Gurtu, A., & Johny, J. (2019). Potential of blockchain technology in supply chain management: A literature review. *International Journal of Physical Distribution & Logistics Management, 49*(9), 881–900.
Gusdorf, V. (2023, October 17). *Behind the scenes—How to rate DLT bonds?* Crypto Assets Conference, Frankfurt am Main.
Guthoff, C., Anell, S., Hainzinger, J., Dabrowski, A., & Krombholz, K. (2023). *Perceptions of distributed ledger technology key management—An interview study with finance professionals.* 2023 IEEE Symposium on Security and Privacy (SP).
Haber, S., & Stornetta, W. S. (1991). *How to time-stamp a digital document.* Springer.
Hafid, A., Hafid, A. S., & Samih, M. (2020). Scaling blockchains: A comprehensive survey. *IEEE Access, 8*, 125244–125262.
Hasan, M., Popp, J., & Olah, J. (2020). Current landscape and influence of big data on finance. *Journal of Big Data, 7*(1), 21.
Hileman, G., & Rauchs, M. (2017). Global blockchain benchmarking study. *Cambridge Centre for Alternative Finance Reports.*
Hofmann, E. (2011). *Supply chain finance solutions.* Springer.

Hofmann, E., Strewe, U., & Bosia, N. (2018). Concept—Where are the opportunities of blockchain-driven supply chain finance? In *Supply Chain Finance and Blockchain Technology* (pp. 51–75).

Hogan Lovells (2023, April 4). *A whole new world—Hong Kong court declares crypto assets are property and can be held on trust*. Retrieved January 12, 2024, from https://www.engage.hoganlovells.com/knowledgeservices/news/a-whole-new-world-hong-kong-court-declares-crypto-assets-are-property-and-can-be-held-on-trust

Huang, J., Chang, K., & Tian, Y. (2019). Analysis of macroeconomic factors affecting the corporate bond yield spread. *Engineering Letters, 27*(1).

Huang, Y.-L., & Shen, C.-H. (2015). The sovereign effect on bank credit ratings. *Journal of Financial Services Research, 47*(3), 341–379.

Iansiti, M., & Lakhani, K. R. (2017). The truth about blockchain. *Harvard Business Review, 95*(1), 118–127.

Juan, A. A., Perez-Bernabeu, E., Li, Y., Martin, X. A., Ammouriova, M., & Barrios, B. B. (2023). Tokenized markets using blockchain technology: Exploring recent developments and opportunities. *Information, 14*(6), 347.

Kapengut, E., & Mizrach, B. (2023). An event study of the Ethereum transition to proof-of-stake. *Commodities, 2*(2), 96–110.

Kasahara, S. (2021). Performance modeling of Bitcoin blockchain: Mining mechanism and transaction-confirmation process. *IEICE Transactions on Communications, 104*(12), 1455–1464.

Kempf, A., & Uhrig-Homburg, M. (2000). Liquidity and its impact on bond prices. *Schmalenbach Business Review, 52*, 26–44.

Khan, D., Jung, L. T., & Hashmani, M. A. (2021). Systematic literature review of challenges in blockchain scalability. *Applied Sciences, 11*(20), 9372.

King, S., & Nadal, S. (2012). Ppcoin: Peer-to-peer crypto-currency with proof-of-stake.

Kohli, V., Chakravarty, S., Chamola, V., Sangwan, K. S., & Zeadally, S. (2023). An analysis of energy consumption and carbon footprints of cryptocurrencies and possible solutions. *Digital Communications and Networks, 9*(1), 79–89.

Kraus, A., & Litzenberger, R. H. (1973). A state-preference model of optimal financial leverage. *The Journal of Finance, 28*(4), 911–922.

Kroll, J. A., Davey, I. C., & Felten, E. W. (2013). The economics of Bitcoin mining, or Bitcoin in the presence of adversaries.

Kugler, L. (2021). Non-fungible tokens and the future of art. *Communications of the ACM, 64*(9), 19–20.

KWG (1998). *Kreditwesengesetz* [German Banking Act]. Bundesgesetzblatt Teil I

Larimer, D. (2013). *Transactions as proof-of-stake.* Crypto Chain University.

Lashkari, B., & Musilek, P. (2021). A comprehensive review of blockchain consensus mechanisms. *IEEE Access, 9*, 43620–43652.

Lavi, R., Sattath, O., & Zohar, A. (2022). Redesigning Bitcoin's fee market. *ACM Transactions on Economics and Computation, 10*(1), 1–31.

Law Commission (2023, June 28). *New recommendations for reform and development of the law on digital assets to secure UK's position as global crypto hub.* Retrieved January 12, 2024, from https://www.lawcom.gov.uk/new-recommendations-for-reform-and-development-of-the-law-on-digital-assets-to-secure-uks-position-as-global-crypto-hub/

Lee, J. (2018). Distributed ledger technologies (blockchain) in capital markets: Risk and governance. *SSRN Electronic Journal*.

Lehmann, M. (2021). National blockchain laws as a threat to capital markets integration. *Uniform Law Review*, *26*(1), 148–179.

Levis, D., Fontana, F., & Ughetto, E. (2021). A look into the future of blockchain technology. *PloS One*, *16*(11).

LFF (2023). *Luxembourg Blockchain III Law to strengthen DLT activity*. Luxembourg for Finance. Retrieved January 12, 2024, from https://www.luxembourgforfinance.com/en/news/luxembourg-blockchain-iii-law-to-strengthen-dlt-activity/

Li, C., & Palanisamy, B. (2020). Eventwarden: A decentralized event-driven proxy service for outsourcing arbitrary transactions in Ethereum-like blockchains. 2020 IEEE International Conference on Web Services (ICWS).

Lin, S. (2023). Proof of work vs. proof of stake in cryptocurrency. *Highlights in Science, Engineering and Technology*, *39*, 953–961.

Liu, Y., Liu, J., Vaz Salles, M. A., Zhang, Z., Li, T., Hu, B., Henglein, F., & Lu, R. (2022). Building blocks of sharding blockchain systems: Concepts, approaches, and open problems. *Computer Science Review*, *46*.

Loncarski, I., & Szilagyi, P. G. (2012). Empirical analysis of credit spread changes of US corporate bonds. *International Review of Financial Analysis*, *24*, 12–19.

Malamas, V., Dasaklis, T., Arakelian, V., & Chondrokoukis, G. (2020). A block-chain framework for increased trust in green bonds issuance. *Journal of Sustainable Finance & Investment*.

May, A. D. (2010). The impact of bond rating changes on corporate bond prices: New evidence from the over-the-counter market. *Journal of Banking & Finance*, *34*(11), 2822–2836.

Mayring, P. (2015). *Qualitative Inhaltsanalyse: Grundlagen und Techniken* [Qualitative content analysis: basics and techniques] (13 ed.). Beltz.

Mayring, P. (2016). *Einfuehrung in die qualitative Sozialforschung: Eine Anleitung zu qualitativem Denken* [Introduction to qualitative social research: A guide to qualitative thinking] (6 ed.). Beltz.

Meiklejohn, S., Pomarole, M., Jordan, G., Levchenko, K., McCoy, D., Voelker, G. M., & Savage, S. (2016). A fistful of Bitcoins: Characterizing payments among men with no names. *Communications of the ACM*, *59*(4), 86–93.

Meuser, M., & Nagel, U. (1991). *ExpertInneninterviews—Vielfach erprobt, wenig bedacht: Ein Beitrag zur qualitativen Methodendiskussion* [Expert interviews—Tried and tested, little thought: A contribution to the discussion on qualitative methods]. Springer.

Michael, A., & Pratt, K. (2023, December 19). *Cryptocurrency statistics 2024*. Forbes. Retrieved January 12, 2024, from https://www.forbes.com/uk/advisor/investing/cryptocurrency/cryptocurrency-statistics/

Mihaljevic, M. J., Wang, L., Xu, S., & Todorovic, M. (2022). An approach for blockchain pool mining employing the consensus protocol robust against block withholding and selfish mining attacks. *Symmetry*, *14*(8), 1711.

Milne, A. (2016). Central securities depositories and securities clearing and settlement: Business practice and public policy concerns. In *Analyzing the Economics of Financial Market Infrastructures* (pp. 334–358). IGI Global.

Mishra, R., Singh, R. K., Kumar, S., Mangla, S. K., & Kumar, V. (2023). Critical success factors of blockchain technology adoption for sustainable and resilient operations in the banking industry during an uncertain business environment. *Electronic Commerce Research*, 1–35.

Modigliani, F., & Miller, M. H. (1958). The cost of capital, corporation finance and the theory of investment. *American Economic Review*, *48*(3), 261–297.

Moeser, M., & Boehme, R. (2015). Trends, tips, tolls: A longitudinal study of Bitcoin transaction fees. Financial Cryptography and Data Security: FC 2015 International Workshops, BITCOIN, WAHC, and Wearable, San Juan, Puerto Rico.

Mokdadi, S., & Saadaoui, Z. (2023). Geopolitical uncertainty and the cost of debt financing: The moderating role of information asymmetry. *Journal of Risk Finance*.

Mori, T. (2016). Financial technology: Blockchain and securities settlement. *Journal of Securities Operations & Custody*, *8*(3), 208–227.

Morrow, M. J., & Zarrebini, M. (2019). Blockchain and the tokenization of the individual: Societal implications. *Future Internet*, *11*(10), 220.

Mortensen, S. F. (2021). The impact of distributed ledger technology on post-trade. *Journal of Securities Operations & Custody*, *13*(4), 320–334.

Moura, T., & Gomes, A. (2017). Blockchain voting and its effects on election transparency and voter confidence. 18th Annual International Conference on Digital Government Research.

Mukherjee, K. N. (2012). Corporate bond market in india: Current scope and future challenges.

Mukherjee, P., & Pradhan, C. (2021). Blockchain 1.0 to Blockchain 4.0—The evolutionary transformation of blockchain technology. In *Blockchain Technology: Applications and Challenges* (pp. 29–49). Springer.

Myers, S. C. (2001). Capital structure. *Journal of Economic Perspectives*, *15*(2), 81–102.

Myers, S. C., & Majluf, N. S. (1984). The capital structure puzzle. *The Journal of Finance*, *39*, 574–592.

Nakamoto, S. (2008). Bitcoin: A peer-to-peer electronic cash system. *Decentralized Business Review*.

Nguyen, C. T., Hoang, D. T., Nguyen, D. N., Niyato, D., Nguyen, H. T., & Dutkiewicz, E. (2019). Proof-of-stake consensus mechanisms for future blockchain networks: Fundamentals, applications and opportunities. *IEEE Access*, *7*, 85727–85745.

Nikolova, S., Wang, L., & Wu, J. J. (2020). Institutional allocations in the primary market for corporate bonds. *Journal of Financial Economics*, *137*(2), 470–490.

Nofer, M., Gomber, P., Hinz, O., & Schiereck, D. (2017). Blockchain. *Business & Information Systems Engineering*, *59*, 183–187.

Nougayrede, D. (2018). Towards a global financial register? The case for end investor transparency in central securities depositories. *Journal of Financial Regulation*, *4*(2), 276–313.

O'Hara, M., & Zhou, X. A. (2021). Anatomy of a liquidity crisis: Corporate bonds in the COVID-19 crisis. *Journal of Financial Economics*, *142*(1), 46–68.

OECD (2019). Initial coin offerings (ICOs) for SME financing.

OECD (2020). The tokenisation of assets and potential implications for financial markets. *OECD Blockchain Policy Series*.

Oh, J., & Shong, I. (2017). A case study on business model innovations using blockchain: Focusing on financial institutions. *Asia Pacific Journal of Innovation and Entrepreneurship, 11*(3), 335–344.

Pana, E., & Gangal, V. (2021). Blockchain bond issuance. *Journal of Applied Business & Economics, 23*(1).

Pass, R., Seeman, L., & Shelat, A. (2017). Analysis of the blockchain protocol in asynchronous networks. Annual International Conference on the Theory and Applications of Cryptographic Techniques.

Perera, S., Nanayakkara, S., Rodrigo, M., Senaratne, S., & Weinand, R. (2020). Blockchain technology: Is it hype or real in the construction industry? *Journal of Industrial Information Integration, 17*.

Perez-Sola, C., Delgado-Segura, S., Herrera-Joancomarti, J., & Navarro-Arribas, G. (2019). *Analysis of the SegWit adoption in Bitcoin.*

Petrasek, L. (2012). Multimarket trading and corporate bond liquidity. *Journal of Banking & Finance, 36*(7), 2110–2121.

Petrov, D. (2019). The impact of blockchain and distributed ledger technology on financial services. *Industry 4.0, 4*(2), 88–91.

Pinna, A., & Ruttenberg, W. (2016). *Distributed ledger technologies in securities post-trading—Revolution or evolution?* ECB Occasional Paper, Issue 172.

Popescu, A.-D. (2020). Transforming capital markets by means of financial digital assets. *Emulations—Revue de Sciences Sociales*(68), 108–119.

Porru, S., Pinna, A., Marchesi, M., & Tonelli, R. (2017). Blockchain-oriented software engineering: Challenges and new directions. 2017 IEEE/ACM 39th International Conference on Software Engineering Companion (ICSE-C).

Prasad, S., Shankar, R., Gupta, R., & Roy, S. (2018). A TISM modeling of critical success factors of blockchain based cloud services. *Journal of Advances in Management Research, 15*(4), 434–456.

Priem, R. (2020). Distributed ledger technology for securities clearing and settlement: Benefits, risks, and regulatory implications. *Financial Innovation, 6*(1), 1–25.

Ratna, T., Abisla, R., Jash, S., Kaushik, A. K., Mishra, S., Padmanabhan, A., Prakash, P., Simons, J., Srikumar, M., & Young, K. (2019). *Blockchain regulation in the United States—Evaluating the overall approach to virtual asset regulation.*

RBA (2023). *About financial market infrastructure.* Retrieved January 12, 2024, from https://www.rba.gov.au/payments-and-infrastructure/financial-market-infrastructure/about.html

Roughgarden, T. (2020). Transaction fee mechanism design for the Ethereum blockchain: An economic analysis of EIP-1559. *ArXiv.*

S&P (2022). *Guide to credit rating essentials.* Standard & Poor's.

Saberi, S., Kouhizadeh, M., Sarkis, J., & Shen, L. (2019). Blockchain technology and its relationships to sustainable supply chain management. *International Journal of Production Research, 57*(7), 2117–2135.

Saguato, P. (2017). The ownership of clearinghouses: When 'Skin in the Game' is not enough, the remutualization of clearinghouses. *Yale Journal on Regulation, 34*, 601.

Saleh, F. (2021). Blockchain without waste: Proof-of-stake. *The Review of financial studies, 34*(3), 1156–1190.

Santo, A., Minowa, I., Hosaka, G., Hayakawa, S., Kondo, M., Ichiki, S., & Kaneko, Y. (2016). *Applicability of distributed ledger technology to capital market infrastructure.*

Santos, J. A. C. (2010). Bank corporate loan pricing following the subprime crisis. *The Review of financial studies, 24*(6), 1916–1943.

Saramago, C. (2022). Using distributed ledger technologies for bond issues—A primer. *Law and Financial Markets Review, 16*(1–2), 43–67.

Schaer, F. (2021). Decentralized finance: On blockchain- and smart contract-based financial markets. *FRB of St. Louis Review.*

Schuster, E. (2021). Cloud crypto land. *The Modern Law Review, 84*(5), 974–1004.

SEC (2013). *What are corporate bonds?* Retrieved from https://www.sec.gov/files/ib_corporatebonds.pdf

SFC (2021). *Ordinance on the Adaptation of Federal Law to Developments in Distributed Ledger Technology.* Swiss Federal Council

Sguanci, C., Spatafora, R., & Vergani, A. M. (2021). Layer 2 blockchain scaling: A survey. *ArXiv.*

Sharma, P., Jindal, R., & Borah, M. D. (2022). A review of blockchain-based applications and challenges. *Wireless Personal Communications*, 1–43.

Shrestha, R., Bajracharya, R., Shrestha, A. P., & Nam, S. Y. (2020). A new type of blockchain for secure message exchange in VANET. *Digital Communications and Networks, 6*(2), 177–186.

Siemens (2023). Siemens issues first digital bond on blockchain. Retrieved January 12, 2024,, from https://www.press.siemens.com/global/en/pressrelease/siemens-issues-first-digital-bond-blockchain

Sompolinsky, Y., & Zohar, A. (2015). Secure high-rate transaction processing in Bitcoin. 19th International Conference on Financial Cryptography and Data Security, San Juan, Puerto Rico.

Soska, K., Kwon, A., Christin, N., & Devadas, S. (2016). Beaver: A decentralized anonymous marketplace with secure reputation. *Cryptology ePrint Archive.*

Sullivan, C., & Burger, E. (2017). E-residency and blockchain. *Computer Law & Security Review, 33*(4), 470–481.

Swan, M. (2015). *Blockchain: Blueprint for a new economy.* O'Reilly Media.

Swathi, P., Modi, C., & Patel, D. (2019). Preventing sybil attack in blockchain using distributed behavior monitoring of miners. 2019 10th International Conference on Computing, Communication and Networking Technologies (ICCCNT).

Szabo, N. (1997). Formalizing and securing relationships on public networks. *First Monday.*

Takaoka, S., & Takahashi, K. (2022). Corporate debt and unconventional monetary policy: The risk-taking channel with bond and loan contracts. *Journal of Financial Stability, 60*, 101013.

Tansey, O. (2007). Process tracing and elite interviewing: A case for non-probability sampling. *PS: Political Science & Politics, 40*(4), 765–772.

Tanwar, S., Parekh, K., & Evans, R. (2020). Blockchain-based electronic healthcare record system for healthcare 4.0 applications. *Journal of Information Security and Applications, 50.*

Tapscott, A., & Tapscott, D. (2017). How blockchain is changing finance. *Harvard Business Review, 1*(9), 2–5.

Tornatzky, L. G., Fleischer, M., & Chakrabarti, A. K. (1990). *The processes of technological innovation.*

Tosh, D. K., Shetty, S., Liang, X., Kamhoua, C. A., Kwiat, K. A., & Njilla, L. (2017). Security implications of blockchain cloud with analysis of block withholding attack. 2017 17th IEEE/ACM International Symposium on Cluster, Cloud and Grid Computing (CCGRID).

Uzsoki, D. (2019). *Tokenization of infrastructure: A blockchain-based solution to financing sustainable infrastructure*. Policy Commons.

Vakta, T., Maheswari, A., & Mohanan, N. U. (2016). *Blockchain disruption in security issuance*.

Valenta, M., & Sandner, P. (2017). Comparison of Ethereum, Hyperledger Fabric and Corda. *Frankfurt School Blockchain Center*, *8*, 1–8.

von Haller Gronbaek, M. (2016). Blockchain 2.0, smart contracts and challenges. *Computers & Law*, *1*, 1–5.

von Soest, C. (2023). Why do we speak to experts? Reviving the strength of the expert interview method. *Perspectives on Politics*, *21*(1), 277–287.

Vukolic, M. (2016). The quest for scalable blockchain fabric: Proof-of-work vs. BFT replication. Open Problems in Network Security: IFIP WG 11.4 International Workshop, Zurich, Switzerland.

Walsh, C., O'Reilly, P., Gleasure, R., McAvoy, J., & O'Leary, K. (2021). Understanding manager resistance to blockchain systems. *European Management Journal*, *39*(3), 353–365.

Wang, G., & Nixon, M. (2021). SoK: Tokenization on blockchain. Proceedings of the 14th IEEE/ACM International Conference on Utility and Cloud Computing Companion,

Wang, W., Hoang, D. T., Hu, P., Xiong, Z., Niyato, D., Wang, P., Wen, Y., & Kim, D. I. (2019). A survey on consensus mechanisms and mining strategy management in blockchain networks. *IEEE Access*, *7*, 22328–22370.

Weerawarna, R., Miah, S. J., & Shao, X. (2023). Emerging advances of blockchain technology in finance: A content analysis. *Personal and Ubiquitous Computing*, 1–14.

Wood, G. (2014). Ethereum: A secure decentralised generalised transaction ledger. *Ethereum Project Yellow Paper*, *151*(2014), 1–32.

Wu, K., Ma, Y., Huang, G., & Liu, X. (2021). A first look at blockchain-based decentralized applications. *Software: Practice and Experience*, *51*(10), 2033–2050.

Yan, S. (2022). Analysis on blockchain consensus mechanism based on proof of work and proof of stake. 2022 International Conference on Data Analytics, Computing and Artificial Intelligence (ICDACAI),

Yang, C.-S. (2019). Maritime shipping digitalization: Blockchain-based technology applications, future improvements, and intention to use. *Transportation Research Part E: Logistics and Transportation Review*, *131*, 108–117.

Yeoh, P. (2017). Regulatory issues in blockchain technology. *Journal of Financial Regulation and Compliance*, *25*(2), 196–208.

Yli-Huumo, J., Ko, D., Choi, S., Park, S., & Smolander, K. (2016). Where is current research on blockchain technology?—A systematic review. *PloS One*, *11*(10).

Zaccaroni, G. (2022). Decentralized finance and EU law: The regulation on a pilot regime for market infrastructures based on distributed ledger technology. *European Papers—A Journal on Law and Integration*, *2022*(2), 601–613.

Zhang, T., Li, J., & Jiang, X. (2021). Supply chain finance based on smart contract. *Procedia Computer Science*, *187*, 12–17.

Zhao, J. L., Fan, S., & Yan, J. (2016). Overview of business innovations and research opportunities in blockchain and introduction to the special issue. *Financial Innovation, 2*, 1–7.

Zhou, Q., Huang, H., Zheng, Z., & Bian, J. (2020). Solutions to scalability of blockchain: A survey. *IEEE Access, 8*, 16440–16455.

Zhou, Y., Soh, Y. S., Loh, H. S., & Yuen, K. F. (2020). The key challenges and critical success factors of blockchain implementation: Policy implications for Singapore's maritime industry. *Marine Policy, 122*.

SPRINGER NATURE

GPSR Compliance

The European Union's (EU) General Product Safety Regulation (GPSR) is a set of rules that requires consumer products to be safe and our obligations to ensure this.

If you have any concerns about our products, you can contact us on ProductSafety@springernature.com

In case Publisher is established outside the EU, the EU authorized representative is:

Springer Nature Customer Service Center GmbH
Europaplatz 3
69115 Heidelberg, Germany

The manufacturer's authorised representative in the EU is Springer Nature Customer Service Centre GmbH, Europaplatz 3, 69115 Heidelberg, Germany. If you have any concerns regarding our products, please contact ProductSafety@springernature.com

Printed and bound by CPI Group (UK) Ltd, Croydon, CR0 4YY
28/09/2026
02224076-0006